With SOE in Greece

Dedicated to the memory of
Patrick Hutchinson Evans 1913–94

A Love-Token
When Dido burned she sang because
Her passion her betrayer was.
He left to wander overseas
And found an empire in the breeze.

I have no empire. But I send,
With music, what can never end,
Something as light as falling dew,
No sea or land can keep from you,

The sea that parted us is twain
For I am coming home again
To hear the music of the spheres:
May this, meanwhile, enchant your ears.

P.H. Evans, 1945

With SOE in Greece

The Wartime Experiences of Captain Pat Evans

Tom Evans

Pen & Sword
MILITARY

First published in Great Britain in 2018 by
Pen & Sword Military
an imprint of
Pen & Sword Books Ltd
47 Church Street
Barnsley
South Yorkshire
S70 2AS

ISBN 978 1 52672 513 4

A CIP catalogue record for this book is
available from the British Library.

Printed and bound in England
By TJ International Ltd, Padstow

Pen & Sword Books Limited incorporates the imprints of Atlas, Archaeology,
Aviation, Discovery, Family History, Fiction, History, Maritime, Military,
Military Classics, Politics, Select, Transport, True Crime, Air World,
Frontline Publishing, Leo Cooper, Remember When, Seaforth Publishing,
The Praetorian Press, Wharncliffe Local History, Wharncliffe Transport,
Wharncliffe True Crime and White Owl.

For a complete list of Pen & Sword titles please contact
PEN & SWORD BOOKS LIMITED
47 Church Street, Barnsley, South Yorkshire, S70 2AS, England
E-mail: enquiries@pen-and-sword.co.uk
Website: www.pen-and-sword.co.uk

Contents

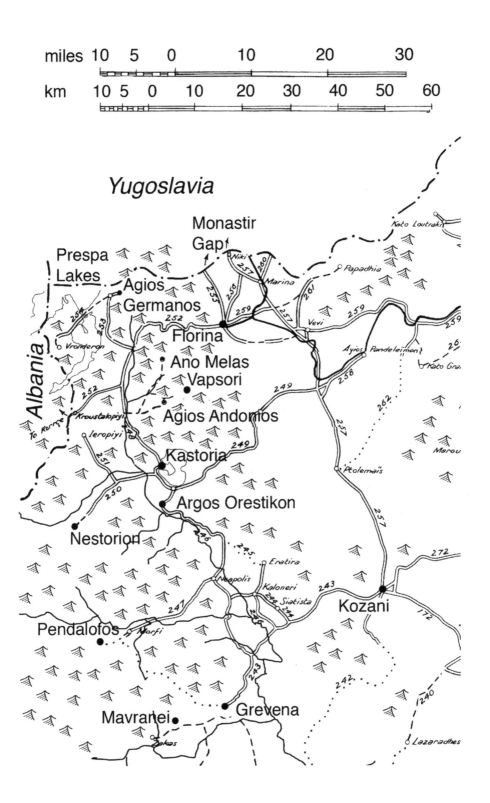

miles 10 5 0 10 20 30

km 10 5 0 10 20 30 40 50 60

Yugoslavia

Monastir
Gap

Kato Loutraki

Niki

Papadhia

Prespa
Lakes

Marina

Agios
Germanos

257 260

255 256 259 257 261

252 259 Vevi 259

Florina

Ano Melas

Vapsori

Ayios Pandeleimon 259

Kato Gra

Albania

254 253

Vronderon

252

249

258 26

262

To Korçe

252

Kroustalopiyi

Agios Andonos

Marou

Ieropiyi

249 257

251

Kastoria

Ptolemais

250

Argos Orestikon

257

Nestorion

246

245

Eratira

272

Neapolis

Kaloneri

243

247 248 Siatista

244

Kozani

172

Pendalofos

Morfi

246

242

243

1240

Mavranei

Grevena

Sakas

Lazaradhes

Foreword and Acknowledgements

In the beginning I knew little about Greece during the Second World War and the civil war that followed, but I was fortunate to be helped and guided by people with an intimate knowledge of the country, the language and the history. My greatest debt, of course, is to my father and principal subject, Patrick Evans. Many of the words, as well as the story, are his. His wartime reports and signals have been widely recognized as essential sources for the study of the resistance in Western Macedonia and the Macedonian autonomist movement. I have also quoted extensively from his wartime diaries and notebooks which are much less well-known, and made use of his private correspondence with his fiancée Jill Rendel, who was to become my mother. The Liddell Hart Centre for Military Archives (hereafter LHCMA) at King's College London holds Pat's wartime papers, and I am grateful to the archivists for their friendly assistance. The private correspondence between Jill and Pat is in my possession.

I have drawn on the SOE files in The National Archives (hereafter TNA) at Kew for Patrick Evans' personnel file, his report to the Foreign Office and signals between the SOE field stations and headquarters in Cairo. Personnel files and reports by other SOE officers also helped to fill in the picture. War Cabinet minutes and papers from 1944–45 (also from TNA) are the primary sources for British strategy and policy towards Greece and the impact of the Greek Civil War on British interests in the Balkans. Kew also provided the RAF records of Pat's landing in Greece. Where I have quoted from archive or published sources, these are referenced in the notes at the end of each chapter. Unless otherwise indicated, unreferenced quotations come from the private correspondence in my possession. Some secondary sources are listed in the Select Bibliography.

The late Sir Geoffrey Chandler, who was one of Pat's colleagues in Greece and became a lifelong friend, was instrumental in starting me on the trail.

It would have been impossible to understand Pat's activities or the nature of the difficulties faced by the mission without following in his footsteps in Western Macedonia. My interviews and discussions with men who knew Pat in Greece provided additional first-hand evidence. I owe a particular debt of gratitude to my companions on three field trips: Howard Rees, Panagiotis Kousoulinis and Athanasios 'Thanassis' Kallianiotis. Without their help, knowledge of the country, its people and their history, I would have got nowhere. Howard was my first guide and mentor. Thanassis not only accompanied my third field trip but also welcomed me in his family home in the village of Aiani, where he and his mother maintained the great Greek tradition of hospitality. Thanassis has been indefatigable in finding answers to seemingly impossible questions and showed me how a real expert goes about gathering oral history. I am also particularly grateful to Professor John Koliopoulos, who introduced me to Panagiotis and Thanassis and made me feel welcome among the historians; his book, *Plundered Loyalties*, was an essential companion and guide of a different kind.

Photographs of personalities and operations in SOE Greece are hard to come by. Most of the officers were not good photographers, were too busy to take pictures and would have relied on local chemists in 'safe' areas to get them developed. I have drawn on Pat's photo album for pictures dating from 1944 and 1945, supplemented by mug-shots from SOE personnel files and a small number of images from other sources.

Four-figure map references in Pat's various reports are based on the 1:100,000 War Office maps of Greece produced by the Geographical Section of the General Staff in 1944. Pat gave his maps to an *Andarte* who served with him; I have used the set held by the London University Senate House library and a 1943 1:500,000 Military Intelligence map of the roads of Western Macedonia from TNA. Comparison between wartime and modern maps of northern Greece shows how much the country has changed. There are many more roads now but many of the villages have disappeared.

English transliteration of Greek place names is variable: Pentalophon, Pentalophos, Pendalofos, Pendalophos and Pentalofos appear in various officers' reports and on maps ancient and modern. Where quoting an English language document directly, I have stuck to the author's transliteration; otherwise I have tried to comply with the usage on modern road maps of Greece. Any errors and inconsistencies are entirely my own fault.

My thanks are due to all the many people in Greece who were so welcoming and helpful to a strange foreigner poking his nose into dark corners of the past. I would like to acknowledge and salute Christos Dalamitros, who worked for Pat as a muleteer during the war, and to thank Toni Gogos, Sakis Goutzinas and Mr Vassilias who helped to trace not only Christos but also Pat's Greek goddaughter Betty.

I would also like to acknowledge the help of all the friends who have read drafts and encouraged me with helpful criticisms and corrections. Finally, my love and gratitude go to my wife Francesca for putting up with my obsessions and distractedness during the years of research, travel and writing.

Glossary

Armies and wars generate acronyms; in northern Greece and the Balkans, the acronyms proliferated wildly as resistance and political groups struggled for power and influence. Sometimes not even the men on the ground were quite sure what an acronym really stood for, or the reality, identity and objectives of the organization or group. Try as one may, the use of unfamiliar acronyms or (transliterated) Greek words is sometimes unavoidable, particularly when they are used in signals, letters and reports. The following glossary spells out an irreducible minimum. Wherever possible, I have used familiar labels such as 'left', 'right', 'nationalist' and 'communist' instead of specific acronyms, taking the view that some over-simplification is better than too much confusion.

AGIS (originally AIS) – Anglo-Greek Information Service: an organization, staffed by British officers and servicemen, set up after the end of the German occupation of Greece to distribute and gather political and economic information and prepare the conditions for democratic elections.

ALO – Allied Liaison Officer: the term used for SOE officers working to support the resistance.

AMM – Allied Military Mission, the SOE organization and operational stations set up to advise and assist the Greek resistance.

Andarte – a Greek resistance fighter.

Ballisti – armed Albanian nationalist bands, supporting the Axis.

Closandarte – an *Andarte* selected and trained to work directly with the British.

EAM – *Ethniko Apeleftherotiko Metopo*, National Liberation Front, the civilian political resistance movement organized primarily by the Greek Communist Party.

EDES – *Ethnikos Dimokratikos Ellinikos Syndesmos*, National Republican Greek League, the largest non-communist resistance organization, with a right-wing nationalist (but not monarchist) leadership.

EKKA – *Ethniki Kai Koinoniki Apeleftherosis*, National and Social Liberation, a small resistance movement opposed by ELAS.

ELAS – *Ellinikos Laikos Apeleftherotikos Stratos*, People's National Liberation Army, the largest armed Greek resistance grouping, which was set up by the Greek Communist Party as the military counterpart to EAM (but included a good many fighters who were not communists).

Force 133 – the code name for SOE Greece.

Fougasse – an improvised mine, dug into a road or bank.

FYROM – 'Former Yugoslav Republic of Macedonia', also referred to in Greece as 'Skopje' after the name of its capital.

Kapetanios – the 'captain' or leader of a resistance group (of any size or political persuasion).

KKE – *Kommunistiko Komma Elladas*, the Greek Communist Party.

Komitadji – an armed village militia of mainly Slav-speaking northern Greeks, set up to support the Axis occupying powers; a member of such a militia.

Ohrana – an Axis-sponsored pro-Bulgarian propaganda organization.

PEEA – *Politiki Epitropi Ethikis Apeleftherosis*, Political Committee for National Liberation: a left-wing 'government-in-waiting' set up in the northern Greek mountains.

Politikos – the political commissar of an ELAS resistance group.

Proedros – elected village headman.

RSR – Raiding Support Regiment, a British Special Forces outfit equipped with heavy weapons, created by HQ Middle East to support SOE, Yugoslav and Greek resistance operations against the German retreat from the Balkans in 1944.

SNOF – *Slavjanomakedonski Narodno Osloboditelen Front*, the Slav-Macedonian National Liberation Front, a left-wing armed resistance movement set up to be a Slav-speaking equivalent of ELAS.

SOE – the Special Operations Executive.

Stratigio – military command centre, headquarters.

Stratiotikos – the military commander of an ELAS resistance group.

Tsipouro – a strong, colourless brandy distilled from the residue of the wine press.

WRNS – Women's Royal Naval Service.

Prologue

Unlocking Memories

As a small boy in the 1950s, I was fascinated by stories of the war and shamelessly pestered my father with questions:

'What kind of gun did you have? Did you have a Sten gun?'

'Yes,' he replied, 'but I didn't like it much. It was hard to shoot straight and hit anything unless you were close.'

'Did you have a pistol?'

'I had a revolver. A good revolver never let you down: you knew that if you pulled the trigger, it would fire, every time. With an automatic, you had to remember to take off the safety catch, and it could jam. Then you would be in trouble.'

'Did you ever shoot a man?'

'I shot at a wolf in the mountains once with a Sten gun, but it ran away.'

This was disappointing. I thought that automatics – and the Luger in particular – looked much more stylish. It was clear that Pat did not like to talk about shooting. To distract me, he reached across the desk and picked up a metal object about as big as his hand. 'Look,' he said, 'this was my parachute release. The parachute was tied to four straps that went round my legs, waist and shoulders. The straps were fixed to these rings, which sat against my chest.' He held it in place. 'When you landed, you had to get out of the harness fast, so you didn't get dragged along the ground. This is how it's done.' Pat turned the metal disk clockwise and slapped it firmly with the palm of his right hand. With a rattle and a clunk, the rings jumped out. 'After that,' he said, 'you packed away your parachute and got moving before the enemy could come looking for you.'

I was too young at the time to understand what Pat had lived through and as the war receded into history, my recollection of Pat's stories became misty and unreliable. His exploits belonged to another life in another time and another place, but Pat kept the parachute release on his desk until he died. After more than seventy years, the mechanism still functioned. The solid, knurled disc is engraved with black letters cut into the grey enamel: 'TURN TO UNLOCK, PRESS TO RELEASE.' The inscription puzzled me. Why was it there? No parachutist could ever forget how the release works and it would be impossible for the wearer to read the instruction when it was in place on his chest. Was the message meant for someone else, perhaps a civilian who might find an injured or unconscious parachutist? If the rescuer could read English, he would not waste time or risk causing further injury by wrestling with the mechanism or trying to cut through the webbing harness. After Pat's death, it seemed like a message, an instruction to open a door into the past.

Three months after the funeral in 1994, my mother Jill called to say that an old letter had turned up describing Pat as a hero for Greek freedom and hoping the British government would reward him. It added to the aura of romance surrounding Pat's wartime activities, but I did nothing.

Six years later, after Jill's death in 2000, I brought home a battered green suitcase full of letters but hardly looked at them; I felt shy about reading my parents' wartime love letters and plans for a family. Finally in 2006, when I was going through family papers, I came across a brown envelope addressed to Jill with a 1994 postmark. Inside, there were carbon copies of two letters sent from the British Consulate General in Salonika in July 1946 to the Foreign Office in London, with a short covering note from Geoffrey Chandler who had worked with Pat in Greece. The old papers were thin, yellow and brittle, held together by a rusted dressmaker's pin; the carbon was fuzzy and uneven, but the letters were clearly legible as follows:

To His Excellency the Minister of War of Great Britain

London

Your Excellency,

We are residents of the North provinces of Greece – the province of Voion – near Mount Pindos – that famous mountain the name of which will always be in your mind, for during the Greek-Italian war there took place the most famous battle of our age, when the small number of Greek soldiers swept away thousands of Italians.

In this province of ours during the dark era of the occupation of Greece by the barbarian conquerors there appeared an officer on the service in H.M.S. famous British Army at the time a Lieutenant of the Commando Unit 133, Mr Evans, having a special mission.

Lt. Evans has been a fine man with a delicate character, self-sacrificing and incomparable heroism, inspired with superior noble ideas, he started for Greece with the intention of fighting for the liberation of our country, no matter if in this way he put himself into sacrifice and danger.

Since the early moments of his arrival here, he was highly appreciated and put in the hearts of all residents of the territories of Voion, Grevena, Kastoria, Vition and Florina, the most important regions where he acted most, considering him as a second Lord Byron.

He proved a restless soldier. He worked night and day under bad atmospheric conditions, wandering together with his collaborators among the many hills and vales, from village to village, having the only aim of doing his duty for his country and the allied Cause.

Besides he proved useful, mild and courteous to all residents. Honour and glory to the country which bears such children.

We, the residents of Voion, who have known and appreciated his goodness and heroism, consider it a great obligation of ours to submit to your Excellency, our kindest desire that be expressed to this man our sympathy and gratefulness to him. On the other hand we would request, if possible, that he be honoured accordingly, being sure that by doing this you would have rewarded one of the most heroic and bravest sons of your Great Country Britain.

Looking forward to a favourable reception of our present petition,

We remain, Honourable Sir,

Yours truly,

(signed) P. GUINIS

Authorized representative of the residents of Province of Voion
Phillipe I. Guinis, P.O. Box 141
Saloniki, Greece, July 4th, 1946.

Some of the references were easy to follow. 'Commando 133' was clearly 'Force 133', the War Office code-name for the Special Operations Executive in the Balkans, directed from a headquarters in Cairo. The SOE grew out of the Secret Intelligence Service (SIS, often known as MI6) in response to the German occupation of continental Europe. A memorandum, signed by Neville Chamberlain as Lord President of the Council on 19 July 1940, recorded that: 'An organization is being established to co-ordinate all action by way of subversion and sabotage, against the enemy overseas. The organization will be known as the Special Operations Executive.' Winston Churchill wrote that its mission was to 'set occupied Europe ablaze'. The SOE was so secret that almost nobody in Whitehall knew of its existence.

'Mount Pindos' (or Pindus) is the great range of mountains that runs through Albania and northern Greece, dividing Epiros from Western Macedonia.

It was easy enough to find out that the district of Voion (or Voio) consists of a scattering of remote mountain villages running from Pendalofos in the west to Siatista in the north. Grevena, Kastoria and Florina are the main towns and administrative centres in this part of Western Macedonia.

The 'most famous battle' took place in November 1940, when an outnumbered Greek force destroyed the Julia Division of the Italian army on the heights of Mount Annitsas.

However, the identity and motives of 'P. Guinis' were mysteries. 'Guinis' clearly knew Pat from his arrival in 1943, referring to him as 'Lieutenant' rather than as 'Captain' (to which he was promoted in February 1944) or 'Major', his rank when he left Greece in 1946. 'People's representative' sounded as if he was a man of the left.

I knew vaguely that the Greek resistance had been split between many different factions, but that the largest – and best-organized – group had been the left-wing People's National Liberation Army, *Ellinikos Laikos Apeleftherotikos Stratos* (ELAS). ELAS had a counterpart civilian organization, the National Liberation Front, *Ethniko Apeleftherotiko Metopo*, known as EAM. ELAS and EAM worked hand in glove and both were effectively controlled, behind the scenes, by the Greek Communist Party, KKE (*Kommunistiko Komma Elladas*). Where did Mr Guinis fit within this network of left-wing political and military resistance organizations? It seemed unlikely that he was a member of the Communist Party, KKE, which had little love for the British 'Monarcho-fascists', although it used British gold and the presence of British Special Forces to bolster its position during the occupation. More plausibly, he could have been a wartime supporter of EAM, possibly even a member of the armed resistance ELAS.

Perhaps he had belonged to some other grouping, or he was just an ordinary villager who belonged to no group at all but suffered almost equally from both the occupying enemy and the resistance? Did he feel gratitude for an act of kindness towards his family and village during the occupation? Was he one of those who sought Pat's protection from the Greek courts after the Germans left, when scores were being settled in the mountains? Would anyone still know after so many years and so much destruction?

In July 1946, when the letter was written, Pat was back in Britain and out of uniform. He had left Greece for good and had no power to influence events or help the writer. Greece was on the brink of a catastrophe: in the autumn of 1946 the country plunged over the precipice and descended into the third and most deadly phase of the civil war, engulfing Western Macedonia in a conflict that devastated hundreds of mountain communities.

The second letter, addressed to the Foreign Secretary in London, had more to say about Pat's activities in Greece:

Sir,

I have the honour to transmit to you herewith a letter addressed by the residents of the district of Voion in the province of Western Macedonia to the 'Minister of War' conveying an expression of their appreciation of the services rendered by Lieutenant P.H. Evans, serving as British Liaison Officer with Force 133. I am forwarding this testimonial to you as I understand Mr. Evans is now working in the French Section of the Press Department of the Foreign Office (former Ministry of Information).

Lt. Evans arrived in Greece in 1943 as British Liaison Officer to the Greek Resistance movement and operated first in the Voion district of Kozani and later in the Northern Pindus (Vitsi) round Florina. His knowledge of the latter area and of the recent revival of the Macedonian autonomist movement there is probably unequalled by any other Englishman. Perhaps the most genuine tribute that can be paid to a man and his work is the sincere respect and great affection that the villagers of these areas now show in their many enquiries after Evans, his present whereabouts and activities. His is a name that will not be forgotten and the popularity of this young and able officer is attested by the enclosed testimonial. He was quick to perceive the Communist affiliations of ELAS and thereby earned himself attacks in the Left-wing press during his subsequent period of service from March 1945 to December 1945 as officer of the Anglo-Greek Information Service at Florina. Mr. Evans took charge of the Press Department of this Consulate-General on its formation in February 1946 and carried out excellent work in the initial organization of the department.

I am sending a copy of this despatch and enclosure to H.E. Ambassador at Athens and enclose carbon copies for transmission to the War Office if desired.

I have the honour to be, Sir,

Your most obedient, humble Servant,

(signed E. Peck) Acting Consul-General

At last I sat down to read Pat's letters carefully. However, the correspondence had long gaps and Pat's letters from overseas were hard to interpret. Even when he could reach a regular postal service, secrecy and censorship prevented him from writing openly about his actions or whereabouts; even his post-war letters from Greece were constrained by official secrecy. I believed that Pat had kept papers from the war, but had found nothing when I cleared the house. However, the online catalogue of the Liddell Hart Archives at King's College London listed three boxes of his papers, signals, diaries, reports and notes. I also found online the text of a secret report he had written for the Foreign Office in December 1944, which had become a reference in the disputes between Greek and Slav claimants to Macedonia's history, culture and territory.

The Liddell Hart Centre for Military Archives supports research into modern British defence strategy and planning. It holds the papers of senior commanders – admirals, field marshals, generals and air marshals – and of SOE officers of any rank. This puzzled me until I realized that, for Churchill and the chiefs of staff, spreading revolt in the German-occupied territories was an arm of strategy. Even small-scale actions by a handful of men in the remote Greek mountains could have an impact on the balance of power in the Balkans and the wider conduct of the war.

In the archives, one can hold and read the raw material of history. The original documents convey the thoughts and feelings of the men and women who wrote them, without mediation or interpretation. Archives may be hushed places of quietly-turned pages and whispered conversation, but the papers in their cardboard storage boxes are full of furious action. They contain the orders that flung armies into battle, desperate memoranda from commanders, diatribes against the caution of civil servants and diplomats, first-hand reports of battles, acts of sabotage and propaganda, tactical and logistical dilemmas, secret signals and accounts for the gold used to finance rebellions or to pay for a night's lodging and a dozen eggs. Those, too, might once have been a matter of life or death for hard-pressed men in enemy territory.

The Liddell Hart Archive is tucked away on the second floor of King's College. Once inside, the crowds of London are shut away and time slows as the past seems to merge with the present. My excitement and anticipation grew as I opened the first box, lifted out a manila folder and untied the buff tape to see Pat's familiar handwriting.

Chapter One

The Journey Out

P at joined up in 1940 and became a tank driver. As he wrote to one of his former schoolmasters, he enjoyed working with tanks: 'The driving entailed unlimited hard work and a good deal of fun too of a grubby but satisfying kind. Compass correction was ticklish but really thrilling – it is always fascinating to deal with, and adapt to your own ends, a force you can neither see, hear, smell or touch.' In 1941 he refused the offer of a commission because, as Jill wrote to her best friend with some exasperation, 'he believes in winning it on the field of battle.' By March 1942, though, he had given in and was at an Officer Cadet Training Unit (OCTU), where he wrote that:

> Life consists of polishing one's boots to a fantastic brilliance and learning about a multitude of things. I have been in the army for over eighteen months and, except that I have been part of Britain's garrison, I have contributed to the war effort exactly nil. I don't feel I am a potential hero but I shall be very glad all the same to get into action. Uselessness is very galling.

From OCTU Pat was sent to the School of Military Intelligence for specialist training. The Intelligence Corps had been founded in 1940 to 'provide for the efficient centralized administration in one corps of personnel employed on intelligence, cipher and censor duties.' By the end of the war it had trained 1,700 officers and other ranks. On the last day of the course at Matlock in Derbyshire, in March 1943, Pat went to see the commanding officer to put forward his ideas about Greece in the hope of getting into Special Operations. They talked about the Greek campaign. 'What about the road from X to Y?' the colonel asked. 'We didn't have time to recce it and were never certain whether the Germans could bring an armoured division down it or not – until they did.' From his memories of a walking trip in 1937 Pat gave him details of the road. 'I wish we had known that at the time,' the colonel said.[1]

Northern Greece was largely unknown territory to the English; apart from the occasional archaeologist, few Englishmen ventured that far from Athens. Pat went there more by accident than design. Having left Oxford without taking a degree, he had spent most of the 1930s knocking around as 'tutor, journalist, publisher's reader, reviewer, secretary, farm labourer', while reading widely and writing poetry. In Paris he had made friends with Henry Miller and Lawrence Durrell. Miller was finishing *Tropic of Capricorn*, the sequel to *Tropic of Cancer*, which had already made him notorious; Durrell was at the outset of his literary career. The Durrell family was living on Corfu and the 11-year-old Gerald needed a tutor. Pat had arrived there to take up the job in 1936, 'a tall, handsome young man fresh from Oxford.'[2]

A photograph from the period shows Pat as a slim figure in jodhpurs and hacking jacket, with a crest of wavy dark hair above a broad forehead and a strong, sharp chin. He is looking down to shade his steely, grey-blue eyes from the sun. Gerald's 16-year-old sister Margo found Pat 'very, very attractive' and became infatuated, to the point where, after a year, Mrs Durrell decided he must leave. Pat made his way to the mainland and walked right across the mountains of Western Macedonia, from Ioannina in the Epirus to Veria in Central Macedonia, just 45 miles from Thessaloniki in the east, before making his way down to Athens.[3] He never talked about Margo (Jill thought he had a bad conscience) but he sometimes told stories about walking in the mountains, where the shepherd dogs wore spiked collars and were almost as savage as the wolves.

After completing his course at Matlock, Pat was posted back to his regiment at Leyburn in Yorkshire, where the wind came sweeping over the moors, 'bounding about the stone house and making it shake'. He was now an assistant Intelligence officer and increasingly frustrated by inaction. On 14 March 1943 he wrote to Jill that

> a job which I want very badly indeed looks like materializing. I applied for it in great fear and trembling at Matlock, was received with open arms, and have lately been told to stand by for a Telegram From The War Office. Very Dennis Wheatley [a best-selling writer of spy stories, who was also a secret intelligence officer]. It's exciting, but this endless waiting is a poor business. 'Any day now' said the last news I had and meanwhile I do a lot of little jobs here, trying to simulate an interest in it all and scan every mail and then wonder how long it will be to the next. Every time I hear footsteps coming along the passage I think, 'Is that the telegram?' and it isn't.

Mugshots in Pat's SOE personnel file show his eagerness and determination. Fortunately, his wanderings in Greece stood him in good stead: Stanley Casson, the CO at Matlock, 'warmly recommended' him to SOE, which was in 'urgent need of Greek speakers and officers with a knowledge of Greece'.[4] Behind the scenes, secret signals had been going back and forth between 'M.O.4' (SOE) in

Cairo, SOE in London and the army to secure Pat's release from the Royal Tank Regiment.

Eventually the telegram came summoning him to London, and on 5 May 1943 he was interviewed by Major Boxshall of SOE. Afterwards Pat took Jill for dinner at Rule's in Covent Garden, and then to her flat in Eton Avenue between Chalk Farm and Swiss Cottage. He left at about 2.30 am and walked for an hour through the blackout, round the Outer Circle of Regent's Park, through the silent, empty streets of Marylebone to Park Lane, where he was staying.[5] Later that day, a note was sent from SOE London to Cairo saying

> due to fortunate and unforeseen developments we have been able to secure the services of 2nd Lieut. P. H. Evans, R.A.C., who was so warmly recommended by Colonel Stanley Casson. Evans was interviewed by us yesterday and found quite promising. Subject to the Security vetting being satisfactory we hope to despatch him to you in the course of this month.[6]

It had been a momentous twenty-four hours. Two evenings later, Pat took Jill for a final dinner before he was swallowed up by the shadowy world of the Special Forces. He could not say where he was going, but he took her to the best Greek restaurant in London, the White Tower in Percy Street. His diary records that they dined on 'soupe karavisha, sole and vegetables for Jill, moussaka, loukmedes. A pleasant red wine, like burgundy, and French coffee.' At the next table, a fat man with a baby face was entertaining. This was Cyril Connolly, a well-known critic who edited the literary magazine *Horizon*. 'After dinner he called for cigars, then when the waiter brought the cigars he turned them down and his guests went without.' At this stage of the war, it was still possible to eat, drink and smoke well in London.

The next day, Pat was back in Yorkshire, preparing for embarkation. Jill had gone to Scotland as a WRNS cipher officer. While they were in London, Pat had committed himself and proposed marriage. Jill had not answered either way, but he was confident and happy. On 13 May, Pat returned to London from Yorkshire to SOE's offices, where he signed the Official Secrets Act. From this moment on, he was 'specially employed' and no longer paid by the army.

Six days later, on 19 May, Pat left the UK for Greece by way of Cairo. He set off like a warrior in romance, cloaked in secrecy, heart full of love for his lady. Strangely, his journey began by travelling directly away from his destination, on a ship that headed far out west into the North Atlantic. Only when safely out of range of patrolling U-boats and aircraft did the convoy turn south into the tropics and then east to the coast of Africa in a 5,000-mile arc that landed him twice as far from his destination as when he started. Pat's letters to Jill, written on board, are undated. Some pages were removed, others mislaid, found and sent on later. Censorship prevented him from writing anything that might have military significance and inhibited him from writing anything very intimate. So he wrote to amuse and to reassure:

> I think of you a great deal and look forward to the day we shall be reunited. If there are any trials and tribulations in front of me I know that I have, in the form of memories of you, a fund of comfort and strength to which I can turn whenever I feel gloomy or harassed… I don't suppose it's a breach of security to say that we can see the Southern Cross. A dainty little constellation. If the Bear is masculine then the Southern Cross is feminine.
>
> Try to console yourself with the thought that the war won't last for ever and that meanwhile you are marvellous – absolutely and wildly and completely impossibly marvellous.

> I have lost count of time and don't know the day or the date. We are fairly near the equator now and it is beautifully hot. A white, sticky heat, but I don't mind it. At night the sea is full of sparks and the whole side of the ship, where it meets the water, is a long ribbon of milky phosphorescence. As our next-door-neighbour ship lifts to a wave you can see her stern all lit up from underneath. It's a lovely sight. This afternoon the sea was swarming with flying fish which kept popping up and gliding gracefully a foot or two above the surface, dipping up and down, like swallows. There was some fish-of-prey, perhaps a small shark, chasing them in a lazy sort of way for some time. We must be getting near land again now, as we see birds again. The only one we have had since the second or third day out was a dainty little falcon, which had strayed hundreds of miles out to sea and stopped for a rest on our mizzenmast. Perhaps it was some southern species of kestrel; I wouldn't know.

> The company on board is quite amusing. Very mixed. Women in quite a minority and very much sought after, in spite of being a very unattractive bevy. People are behaving in a way that makes me think Somerset Maugham must be true after all.
>
> The first week of the voyage was lousy. The sea was choppy and I felt extremely bilious and had a headache though I wasn't sick; so did a lot

of others (including some naval officers, which reassured me) and we all told each other we were feeling fine, thanks old chap, bit stuffy on board though wasn't it – and went on eating our meals out of sheer vanity and in the utmost discomfort. But my stomach soon made friends with the ocean and then the weather got warm, and now life is idyllic.

There is an Irish girl aboard who apparently has been 'misbehaving' herself, whatever that may mean – heaven knows what adulteries on the boat deck. After all it's the heat, what, don't you know? I always say, old man, a fellow can't be a plaster saint, what? (We have some Empire-builders on board.) So a posse of the male passengers, in a mixture of hilarity and a sort of uneasy morality, dash-it-the-girl-did-go-a-bit-too-far sort of thing – altogether most odd – decided one evening to tie her in her bunk to keep her out of mischief, ha-ha! (Lots of whatting and don't-you-knowing at this point; whispered conferences in the saloon etc.) The girl got wind of it and instead of hiding herself in a lifeboat or taking sanctuary somewhere, she went down to her cabin, put on her best nightdress, overhauled her complexion with great care and lay on her bunk. And was duly tied to same.

My sweet/I think the waw/Is a baw/Because of security/I have to wrap all my movements in the darkest obscurity.

And it is a baw because I can now say that I have finally seen the tropics for the first time and they are very exciting. And I want to tell you all about it. They haven't let me down a bit. They always seemed so wonderful in Conrad and other writers that I couldn't quite believe it was true. Well it is. They are pestiferous but lovely.

At the risk of making you burst with envy let me tell you that I have been eating fruit. Pineapples running with juice, and little green bananas which are ripe although they don't look it. I also have an avocado pear which I am going to eat in a few minutes. It is dark greeny-purple and shaped like a walnut with the rind on, and about the size of a cricket ball; its inside is filled with pale green shaving cream. I also have some oranges but I haven't got round to eating them yet.

I have been talking to Empire-builders. Very cautiously. One has to stalk them with stealth and cunning and make sure of selecting the right one as some of them are crashing bores. By and large they are some of the oddest people I have ever met... but many of them are worth meeting – for their unusual angles on existence, for their accounts of the fantastic overheated places in which they live and rule or trade; and even when they are bores for their sheer oddness; good additions to one's mind's collection of human beings.

The censor objected to part of the next letter, which begins in mid-sentence:

...passengers, ranging from three little blackamoors (one couldn't call them Negroes, they were too much like the picaninnies one used to see in storybooks in one's childhood) to some moth-eaten but elevated Naval officers. A fair sprinkling of women – mostly rather mousey and some dreary to the nth. And one Freddy Ayer, a former philosophy don from Oxford who writes for *Horizon* and knows Stephen Spender and many others from the menagerie of our acquaintances and semi-acquaintances in that and similar circles. He is a witty and intelligent person with large eyes like a jerboa, a large triangular head and a small body. He is good fun and it is great luck to have bumped into him as an addition and companion for a voyage. John [Cook] is nice but sticky; an awful old woman sometimes. The objects of these descriptions are sitting in armchairs next to me, all unconscious, and I feel rather like a Judas. Freddy [Ayer] is reading *The Amberley Papers*[7] which he says are fascinating and which I am going to read after him.

John Cook, who had been recruited along with Pat from the Intelligence course at Matlock by Colonel Casson, was a classical scholar and archaeologist who became Director of the British School at Athens after the war and then a professor at Bristol University. A.J. 'Freddie' Ayer was an agent for both SOE and MI6. The publication of *Language, Truth, and Logic* in 1936 had made his reputation as a philosopher and he went on to become Wykeham Professor of Logic at Oxford. Stephen Spender was already established as a leading poet and essayist, and later became Poet Laureate.

The letter continued:

At the port John and I didn't have to queue and fiddle around with the rest of the passengers; there was an Army officer waiting for us, who simply took us through all the controls in front of everyone else as if we had been a couple of prima donnas. Most agreeable. I was sorry for the people who did have to queue but glad all the same to be treated as a privileged person.

I suppose if I say anything at all about the port and this ship and the convoy it will be blacked out by the censor, so I will confine myself to saying

1. It is a reasonably comfortable ship; the food is excellent but it is hard to get a bath; the War Dept does us proud and sends us First Class, with the best of everything.
2. Gin and lime costs 8d [a bit over 3p] and cigarettes are 2/- [10p] for 50!
3. The sea is grey and placid and the convoy moves so slowly that the ships, of which there is a large flock, show hardly any bow wave. This gives the illusion that we are not moving at all; a curious un-peaceful sensation of being stuck for good between earth and sky; everything seems unreal, including the people I am with. (This is something to do with you. I feel I have left my real life behind in London.)
4. There are two dreadful little French women on board…and two very patriotic Wrens… But there is also a Naval Sub-Lieut who plays the piano exquisitely – Bach, Scarlatti, Handel and the like.
5. I was on A[nti]A[ircraft] watch this afternoon in a small pen of steel and concrete right on top of the ship, with a twin machine gun. Just the ships and the toy guns and the sunny silvery sea for company. It was the first time for two years that I haven't felt in a hurry – the pressure of the near future always in one's mind. I loved the monotony of it. Towards the end it rained and I was glad to be relieved. The next man took part in a practice AA shoot – all the ships in the convoy crackling and popping away, just to give their guns a pipe-opener. A fine sight. Curious how pale the sparks of guns look in the daylight.

The Atlantic is a very dull ocean…. End of voyage. I see I never finished this letter but began another one instead.

John Cook remembered that he and Pat disembarked at Lagos, where they were lodged by the Ministry of Economic Warfare and had a few days to look around and relax. On 25 June 1943 Pat wrote again to Jill:

The garden is full of bulbuls (rather like a thrush but sweeter-voiced). Other birds are so bright they simply are not true – there is one with a purple back and wings, an orange skullcap and the rest of it a more vivid crimson-scarlet than could ever be described in words or depicted by paint.

We resume our wanderings sometime soon, I believe. I have heard a lot about a place called Kano in Northern Nigeria – in the great grass belt which runs across Africa, south of the desert and north of the bush. It's a marvellous ancient walled city.

I spent last Sunday surf-riding, in warm surf and the company of an ancient but sprightly General, who was amusing.… The tropical night, which is inky black and starry and full of distant thunder and the shrilling of crickets, is making my mood black as well. I should have double the fun if you were here.

The next stage was made by air, from Lagos north-east to Kano, across the desert to Khartoum and then up the Nile Valley. The RAF had established a 3,500-mile supply route that started on the coast at Takoradi and went through Accra (Ghana), Lagos and Kano (Nigeria), Fort Lamy (now called N'Djamena, in Chad), El Fasher (Darfur), Khartoum and Wadi Halfa (Sudan) to Cairo. As Pat wrote: 'It was an amazing journey.'

On the way, Pat got his wish to see Kano:

We cycled through it before dinner, three of us. Innumerable narrow streets between low mud buildings of a quasi-Moorish style; donkeys, goats, horses, sheep etc. through which we threaded our way with much jingling; the people were fine and upstanding, courteous, but didn't really give a damn for us, which was refreshing; among other things we passed a Mohammedan school which consisted of about two dozen little black boys in loin cloths or nothing at all, sitting cross-legged in the dust and sun, chanting the Koran with happy grins on their faces; in the middle of them sat the teacher in a turban and spectacles and white robes, leading the chant and looking about in a bored kind of way.

Our guide was a corporal of the Emir's police, dressed in a uniform of royal-blue jodhpurs and tunic with crimson facings and a crimson turban. It is impressive to find because I have two pips on my shirt I get a salute and an un-servile obedience from people like this; and of course it's a great help to be sailed along, the corporal alternately cursing and greeting the population as we pushed through the throng. He had a big bass voice and was royal enough to be an emir himself. Once he very expertly lashed out and gave a sleepy goat a flying kick in the ribs with his sandaled foot as he passed by; and the goat moved about an inch to the side and took no further notice (that's Africa). After we had viewed the outside of the Emir's palace, which was a large walled place consisting of courtyards and courtyards, the corporal left us; I went up to a young constable on duty who looked like a prince and asked him how we would get out of this labyrinth of a city (in pidgin: 'This road he go for gate outside city?') and he stood squarely to attention and threw up a smashing salute and said 'Yes, sar!' – so the least I could do was throw up the most impressive Sandhurst salute in return; after which we proceeded in a stately manner on our way, with much jingling of bicycle bells, and found the gate without difficulty...

When we got out of the city we had about two miles to go before reaching the transit camp. We crossed an open space which was evidently a market: there were hundreds of cattle with enormous horns, humps and dewlaps; the natives used a kind of lasso. The horsemen were lovely; they wore very dignified and flowing white robes and their saddle cloths were of several colours; the bridles and reins were gaudy; the horses were dainty beasts, finely built, long-striding little Arabs, rather fiery, and their riders sat them beautifully. It is over such fine and dignified people that the English have the impertinence to rule in shorts! And on the whole we appear to rule pretty well.

A few days later, Pat was on the banks of the Nile, far from the humidity of the Gold Coast and Nigeria:

The air is marvellously dry and light and brilliant. I can only describe the sunlight here by saying that it is solid. I suppose this is the tropical zone at its best.

The bush, which was the first type of African scenery I saw, was beautiful, frighteningly thick and prolific, and unhealthy in the extreme.

Where we were a little time ago the air was wet; the temperature by day was only about 80°, a little less by night, but it felt too hot and once in an armchair it was an effort even to cross the room for a cigarette or a book. The sun shone rarely and even when it did it had mostly to force itself through a hazy gap in the rainclouds. African thunderstorms – which are of a grandeur quite unknown to the English variety – were always lounging about somewhere near, and there was a heavy tension always in the air. The vegetation was – I don't know how to describe it – well it just overflowed and poured over everything like the top of a glass of beer which has been filled too full. The bird and insect life was as vivid as you would expect. The bush was only a hundred yards way: juju and talking drums and palm wine and witch doctors were all there, and quite genuine. Meanwhile we had the radio and electric light. Abrupt contrasts between our own up-to-date technical civilization and the timeless, senseless and fascinating African way of life thrust themselves upon one's notice at every turn. While I was there a two–year–old boy was cured by a witch doctor of what the local hospital had diagnosed as bronchial pneumonia....

Here we are in the dry tropics and the colours are few and pale but pleasant. We have the desert on either side of us and a narrow strip of palm trees and gardens and crops along each bank of the Nile. Which latter varies from bluish to grey to brown to green in colour – we had a curious view of it from above as our very large aircraft came slowly tilting down to land – the towns and gardens and rivers and bridges and desert slanting and revolving, absurdly small and toy-like. Indeed I think it's the dislocation of one's sense of proportion above all that makes air travel an experience as well as a convenience. A whole continent becomes a mere toy – and yet remains as vast as before. One covers untold distances – and yet as one looks down through the porthole one realizes: 'If I were to be dumped down just here by parachute I should be done for.' I should be sheltering in the non-existent shade of *that* bush; or I should climb to the top of *those* completely barren hills to get an all-round view; and it wouldn't make any difference that this ground has been covered by caravans for twenty or forty centuries; those vultures which I can now see below us would be above me and start following and I should start going off my head from thirst and probably last four or five days, not more. Meanwhile here we are miles from anywhere, roaming along in the blue in perfect serenity.

From the ground the desert is a very pale cream colour with occasional variations but from the air you see that it is mottled like the marbled cover of an old-fashioned library edition or an account book. You hardly ever see a living thing except vultures, let alone a human being, yet you see innumerable traces of human beings having been there at one time or another – caravan tracks, little patches of abandoned cultivation (presumably near former springs), occasional cairns and so on. The wadis are all dry and look like cracks in the earth's skin, parched as it is by the wind and sun. Very jagged and spectacular hill ranges rise up out of the surrounding flatness like the foreshortened hills on a relief map, and when you pass near these the aircraft bumps up and down as if it was being hit by something palpable. It is at once boring and fascinating. It is all the same but you can't help looking at it.

The temperature here by day is over 100° in the shade. You can't take liberties with it but the air's so pure and good that you feel equable and gay. Physical laziness and mental activity.

I wish I knew even half the names of the shrubs and trees I have seen, both in the gardens and out of them. Frangipani, bougainvillea, oleander and canna are the only ones I can call to mind; of course there were several kinds of palms as well. (Outside the window of the room I am to sleep tonight there are four date palms turned into albinos by the electric light; the sky is dark behind them and the stars are enormous…)

A slice of lime is even better with fish than a slice of lemon and it leaves a beautiful smell on the fingers after you have squeezed out the juice. One of the best drinks in the world is *fresh* limejuice with soda water, a little gin and a lump of ice. We have been eating bananas, oranges, pawpaws and grapefruit.

We have seen countless queer creatures – e.g. the African crown bird, a small crane with a head like Prince Ras Monolulu [a racing tipster, who pretended to be a Falasha prince and wore a flamboyant headdress] and here in the Nile ibises and pelicans. At a desert airfield where we spent the night there was a tame gazelle, a pretty little creature, friendly and very clean – like a new kid glove. Their previous pet was a lion but it got bored with them and went away.

On 4 July 1943, the flight ended: Pat had arrived in Cairo.

6 July 1943

This is a city of skyscrapers and beggars. It's beginning to get hold of me a little. Shoeblacks and paperboys make a dart at you every few yards. Donkey-carts and lackadaisical spidery cabs, with Arab horses, crowd the streets; so do large American streamlined cars with terrific horns. The sun is hot at half-past seven: it forces one out of bed. The squares are circular and have clusters of very orderly palms in the middles – the straight thick kind not the leaning graceful ones I have seen on the edge of tropical lagoons. Semi-oriental music in quartertones, monotonous but rather exciting, wriggles out of the doorways of flyblown little cafés in side streets. The poorer shops have no fronts: they are like recesses or theatre stages where the shopkeeper plus two or three customers plus several relations sit in a huddle for hours, talking, with tarbooshes on, and nobody does very much. Prices are fantastic. There are troops everywhere. There is a bright green tree which lines many of the boulevards and which keeps horizontal sheets of orange flame in vistas in front of you. The whole place is a congeries, a magnificent vital debased huddle of contrasts – ancient and modern and fake modern. The donkeys wear necklaces of sky-blue beads against the evil eye. The blocks of flats are enormous and successfully streamlined like the cars. Yesterday I found a little barber's shop which looked like a cardboard model or a rather tame cubist picture: its name, in solid Gill Sans chromium-plated letters, was L'ART CAPILLAIRE. Most of the women are sticky-looking and over-adorned, like cakes in a confectioner's window; some are works of art; some wear tribal clothes and net veils and have golden noses and faces speckled with tattooing.

I am well and busy.

I'm so glad you told your parents about our getting married and that they like the idea.... (I highly approve of your vision of a garden full of perambulators and I trust your mind will go on running on these lines.)

After a few days in Cairo, Pat flew 300 miles to a base in Haifa, on the Mediterranean coast of Palestine, to continue his training. At Haifa, he undertook SOE's 'paramilitary training' course, which set the pattern for all subsequent commando and Special Forces training. Here he learned the skills of jiu-jitsu and unarmed combat, silent killing, carrying out and resisting interrogation, sabotage with explosives, night operations in wild country, and how to scale a sheer wall with no hand or footholds. He enjoyed it thoroughly.

14 July 1943

I am getting an inordinate amount of exercise and thriving on it – eating a lot, sleeping like a child and going salmon-pink in some places and brown in others from the sun. I have been bathing. It is hot – very – but I don't seem to mind. I'm living in a tent with a concrete floor; there is, fortunately, a breeze most of the day which comes in puffs over the maize fields and orchards. As the tent is endways on to the wind one has to tether everything and even then something is always flying away and the place looks like a haystack and one can never find one's comb, shirt, shorts, etc. Still it's good fun; a pleasant, thoughtless life. John [Cook] is still with me. He moves about in a one-piece because of stiffness and sunburn, and looks rather dead and pink like a boiled prawn. I expect he will be better in a day or two.

Pat was having an exciting time in training, although he could write nothing about it; his letters home were filled with incidentals. Days were hot and clear; on one exercise, he was able to bathe 'in a freshwater pool in some very barren hills'. Nights were warm, with 'enormous stars, also crickets and fireflies' and, after sunrise, the maize fields smelled of honey.

23 July 1943

Yesterday we finished a course and we had a magnificent celebration. It is a long time since I enjoyed an exclusively male party so much. Liquor flowed in rivers… It was a marvellous party; one realized again how grand people are…

I had a minor accident a couple of days ago and wrenched both knees rather badly. At first I was in a panic because I thought I had slipped at least one cartilage – and that's a job that entails endless operations, sometimes unsuccessful, and messing about and general stagnation. But it's nothing worse than a strain and I'm very much relieved. In a week or two I shall be absolutely all right again and meanwhile I can already walk instead of hobbling. Both my knees are bulging with bandages and I look ridiculous….

Thank you for being so patient and writing to me so often; it means a lot. My letters to you are empty I know; but the days are gone when friends of mine abroad used to write to me in England with profuse descriptions of where they were and what they were up to. Partly because security in general has tightened up, partly because they were Other Ranks and now I'm an officer.

In addition to paramilitary training, Pat was taking the SOE parachute course at the RAF base on Mount Carmel, and had landed heavily after one jump. In 1943, parachutists were members of a small élite. RAF Squadron 148 dropped SOE operatives and their supplies into the Balkans from specially-adapted Halifax long-range heavy bombers. Parachuting from low level at night over rough mountain country was a hazardous and nerve-wracking business. Getting out of the aircraft and into space through the 1-metre hatch cut in the floor of the bomber was practised over and over in a section of fuselage on the ground. The trainee was not allowed in the air until the drill had become automatic. Pat was fortunate; his knees recovered quickly and he completed the programme of day and night drops, from progressively lower heights, that qualified him to wear the parachutist's wings.

Pat took detailed notes from his course on the use of explosives for demolitions and sabotage and, much later, wrote that

it gave a first-rate introduction to the subject for those of us who knew nothing about it…. But there was one very weak spot in the course. Instruction seemed to have been based on northern Europe and the targets to be found there, though we were going to south-east Europe, where the terrain is mountainous and the targets are mainly not industrial:

by far the commonest demolition we carried out, in my own area at least, was blowing roads and masonry bridges. Almost nothing was said about blowing roads – which is a tricky business and demands a good knowledge of the various conditions and obstacles one is likely to meet.... In blowing roads we made one or two mistakes which a little instruction beforehand would have enabled us to avoid.[8]

At Haifa, Pat met soldiers who had volunteered to return to fight behind the lines in their homelands. He discussed the political situation in Greece with officers who had escaped after the Germans overran the country in 1941. On 2 August, Pat noted in his diary:[9]

Told to me by Greek officers in the last few days: 'Greece will never go Communist in the first place because she is not by nature a communistic or potentially communistic country, in the second because the Greeks know that Communism comes from Russia and that the Russians as Slavs are likely to be in with the Bulgars.' ... but another officer says that Communism in Greece is a real danger and 'the situation is as critical as it was in Russia in 1917.' The attitude and understanding of Great Britain will be one of the deciding factors. The Greek people as a whole do not understand what Communism is; nor do they understand a different thing, what Socialism is, but poverty and ignorance combined might detonate a wave of Communism in Greece. Another said that the Greeks and Yugoslavs were like brothers, they were the same kind of people and mostly the same religion.

Each was right, in his way, about the political cauldron of northern Greece.

6 August 1943

The other day, or night rather, I took part in a night scheme and made an awful mess of it and lost my way – worst of all I was the only one to do so. I wandered about for hours and hours and finally returned very dejected to this place, only to be refused entry by the guard. I had left my pass in my room before setting out and had absolutely no proof of identity. I should explain that the guards out here are very strict and effective: our sentries shoot you or stick a bayonet into you on very little provocation. (I'm not exaggerating, believe me. Several people have been damaged by them recently.) Having argued for a long time to no effect, I walked up the road a little way and sat down and thought. I was very tired. I decided that a night in bed was worth two in the bush, or the local equivalent of same. So with infinite stealth and a considerable amount of physical difficulty I got in *sub rosa* without being spotted. This required much more skill than the rather potty night-exercise, which I had taken too easily. I went to bed pleased with myself, feeling that my blunders were redeemed. If the guard had spotted me I should certainly have been attacked and I shouldn't have stood any chance at all. Setting nightlines in the New Forest, and various illicit expeditions with Jim Ballard [an NCO in the 50th Royal Tank Regiment] must have stood me in good stead. The other people who had been on the exercise were full of jokes at my expense the next day, but had to admit that what I had done was much more difficult than the exercise itself.

(2 September 1943, from Cairo)

Some time ago I and a number of others were scrambling up and down some barren rocky thorny hills, largely to keep fit. It being very hot we used to walk all night and lie up in the daytime under the olives. Arabs also travel by night with strings of camels which have fabulous, snooty faces and are led by two or three men on tiny donkeys. The men sing little snatches of Arab songs – those caterwaulings that sound awful on the wireless but which suddenly make sense (apart from the words, which one doesn't know) when one hears them in the hot silvery night, with every star in heaven unusually brilliant and all the crickets in the world singing away fortissimo. One night, quite early on when we still had the better part of twenty miles to go before morning, we saw the cheerful glare of a bonfire on the edge of a village and decided to call there for water. We found a family, about twelve strong, various relationships, squatting in easy attitudes on a rough terrace. Arabs have a childlike and noble hospitality and before we could say anything much they had whisked a great pile of mattresses and hard oblong cushions out of the house and arranged us on them like kings. Watermelons were brought and artfully cut up and with incessant smiles and encouragement we were forced to eat about a melon each, as well as grapes. I was attended by a boy who personally prepared each slice of melon before handing it to me: he did everything except put them in my mouth and watched my every movement. There were grapes too. Then we were brought a drink we didn't recognize at first: it was pure coffee (Arabic 'gaweh') roasted

I think rather green and made without sugar. It had a pleasant bitter taste and was twice as refreshing and stimulating as any other coffee: it cleaned your tongue and put a definite new staying power into you. They couldn't make too much fuss of us and it was a wild beautiful scene in the firelight. The women kept the fire going, not the men, with straw: they were boiling something in a big black cauldron. When at last we tore ourselves away we were so zipped up by the coffee and so tanked up with water in the form of melon that we walked like anything for miles.

Pat returned from Haifa to Cairo in a more positive state of mind. His letters contain a mixture of comments about family and friends, reflections on the possibilities of post-war life, and observations of the city around him.

24 August 1943

Am back now where I was before, but this time in a better temper – not swearing at the traffic, heat, etc. Partly because a) I am now in a suburb and b) the place I have come from was a good deal hotter than this and there were no amenities, the routine was a bore and the people in charge were stooges. Now I am back in civilization with John Cook and John Mulgan.

Mulgan was a New Zealander who had graduated from Oxford with a first in English and had the beginnings of a reputation as a serious literary figure. The three men were all soon to be parachuted into Greece; Pat's diary mentions a dinner conversation in which they discussed the recent escape of a British officer from Poland.

ই

29 August 1943

For the first time I have been in a good enough temper to notice how beautiful and queer this city is. It's a curious city: the atmosphere is strange, because the Egyptians are not a nation but just a lot of people – an important difference. I suppose they must have some underlying unity and fondness for each other yet one feels that what matters here is the individual not the community. The little affair of the moment, not any large trend of movement in society. These Egyptians have been enjoying life and swindling one another and enduring the exploitation from their own rich men for so many centuries that they have worked it all out into a casual, idle *modus vivendi*, rich in sensations, which presumably never will change because, in the first place, it works and in the second the climate is luxuriously hot, too hot for us, relaxing, the sort of air and atmosphere which make you sit and watch and laugh rather than get up and do. And in the third place their way of life is a habit.

ॐ

3 September 1943

So it'll have to be at some future date I tell you the *p'tits détails* of Cairo, the little things one sees – the pseudo acacias with flame-coloured blossom (and one enormous genuine with blue flowers) and a house covered with birdcage on ramshackle balconies labelled ___ ___ *Oiseleur d'Egypte Vente et Achat d'Oiseaux Rares* and the funerals (everybody keening and throwing themselves about as they carry the coffin through the streets but obviously having a thoroughly good time).

ॐ

5 September 1943

I can't tell you what I am doing, except that it is quite uneventful and takes me to an office most days. I expect to get a lot of work someday soon and you'll probably only hear from me once a fortnight or so, and don't be alarmed if you don't hear even that often. And don't be afraid that I shan't take care of myself – I do and am flourishing....

The difference between a small boy and a grown man is small, much smaller than it appears, a fact which cuts all sorts of ways. I think very few of us are really grown-up. One of the sidelights of this fact is the way young writers of the same age as ourselves…have always been so expert about everything – one feels they have never quite outgrown the sixth form of their prep schools.

My mental exercise has consisted of Modern Greek; I get tired of reading tripey newspapers just for the language's sake, and have been reading instead the Apocalypse, an amazing piece of work, which shows a sense of the dead which is Egyptian rather than Greek or Jewish.

ॐ

14 September 1944

I am leading an interesting life in a fine climate and am no longer feeling frustrated. I got your letters on my return from a strenuous, exceedingly interesting week, ten days rather, spent mainly in walking a large number of miles with my first command.

Jill was not to receive this letter, or any others from Pat, for nearly six months. Final preparations were under way. Pat flew from Cairo to the RAF base at Tocra, over 700 miles south-west in Cyrenaica. At 19.55 on the evening of 15 September, a Halifax Mk2 of 148 Squadron took off on Operation COACHMAN 34 to deliver him to Greece, over 1,000 miles to the north. On the first pass over the drop zone, the reception party failed to reply to the code signal of the letter of the day; they tried again and eventually, a little before midnight, all was well and from a height of 1,100ft Pat parachuted into Greece.[10] His General Report recorded laconically:

> Dropped at MASTROYANNI with Capt (now Maj) WINLAW, Bdr (now S/Sgt) KITE, and Cpl PHOTOPOULOS. After delivering stores to the station at KASTANIA, who sent down a party to collect them, our own party travelled to PENTALOPHON with a convoy of about 10 mules.[11]

In a notebook, he described the experience of the drop:

> The moonlight was brilliant. The aeroplane circled three times round the mountain as if it was describing a contour. When it had done three quarters of the third circle it slowed down – suddenly, alarmingly, and sickeningly. It had slowed down just as much the other two times but it hadn't felt like that.
>
> Photopoulos, with his parachute strapped to his back, sat on the edge of the large round hole in the floor with his legs dangling in the air. He and I gazed down at what we could see, through the hole, of his native land. It consisted at this point of jagged rocks and boulders, dotted with small black bushes. The worst possible ground for parachutists to land on.
>
> The aircraft was so low that the ground looked almost as close as from the window of a slowly moving train. Suddenly I became conscious of all sorts of tiny details. Out of a corner of my eye I caught the rosy glow of the warning light for dropping. The dispatcher shouted 'Action

stations – go!' Photopoulos, fumbling a little, dropped out of sight with a rush of wind and a sound like the crack of a whip and, mechanically, I too began fumbling into position on the edge of the hole. I pressed my feet together, slipped through the hole with my scalp full of gooseflesh.

I seemed to fall vertically for a long time. Then the slipstream gave me a sideways shove through space; the world became luminous and fresh; with a slight but peremptory tug my parachute opened. All my anxiety dissolved as I found myself floating safely in the cold, sweet air.[12]

Chapter Two

Boodle

Pat had dropped into Greece on a mountainside not, as the letter had suggested, in the Pindus mountains but far to the south, on the western edge of the Thessaly plain, on a mountainside near a village that has since been renamed 'Amarantos'. The mission station to which he was assigned, at Pendalofos in Voion, was a long march away, over 100 miles of mule tracks northwards through the mountains, avoiding the German-dominated roads in the valleys and plain.

As they approached their destination, Pat's group passed across a series of steep valleys, rich with the colours of early autumn. The beeches were turning to copper while the oak trees were still lush and green. A little river cut its bed through strata of sandstone and shale, which had weathered into a fantastic mass of snaking, bulging tubes. Just outside the village, the mule track crossed the river on a steep stone bridge that spanned the river with a single high, semi-circular arch.

The village itself sat at an altitude of 1,040 metres on the flanks of Mount Voion, surrounded by chestnut trees. Pendalofos was, in those days, a large and prosperous village by the standards of Western Macedonia. Before the war, it had more than 1,700 inhabitants, with its own police station, Post Office and school. Pendalofos was known locally as a village of stonemasons: hundreds of two- and three-storey stone houses huddled picturesquely around the mountain. Village life was hard and primitive, little changed for hundreds of years. Walls were whitewashed every year to kill the bugs, mules were used for transport and haulage, women still wore traditional costumes that can now only be found in museums, people believed in the evil eye, and the ancient customs of hospitality were sacrosanct. In the square at the centre of the village, a great beech tree formed a focal point for gatherings, speeches and celebrations.

The SOE's base in Pendalofos had only been set up the month before, on 10 August 1943, by an advance party of two British and one Greek officer (Captain Prentice, Captain Wickstead and Lieutenant Zotos) who, like Pat, had dropped at Mastroyanni to avoid the 'Hun threat' to any site further north.[1] Now, in September, it was established as the headquarters of the Military Mission in Western Macedonia and the command centre of the Ninth Division of ELAS, the left-wing 'National People's Liberation Army'.

ELAS was the largest of the resistance groups in Greece, with about 15,000 guerrillas under arms, 6,000 of them in Western Macedonia. ELAS went hand in glove with its sister organization EAM, the 'National Liberation Front'. In the background, pulling the strings of both ELAS and EAM, was the Greek Communist Party, KKE. Although the connection was not universally understood, even in the ranks of the resistance, it was the communists who directed the policy, strategy and tactics of both EAM and ELAS. EAM's role was to organize civilian life and set the political direction for the armed resistance. The command structure of the military wing, ELAS, reflected the twin military and political aims of the left-wing resistance. Every unit from the platoon to the 'supreme command' had three commanders: the *kapetanios*, who was the leader, a political commissar (*politikos*) who gave orders and a military commander (*stratiotikos*) who carried them out. It was not always clear to the liaison officers where the real power and authority lay: the *stratiotikos* would have previously served with the Greek armed forces, and although nominally a commander was often a figurehead. Ostensibly, the political commissar was just a liaison officer, communicating with the civil authorities. In reality, he was appointed by EAM to direct ELAS's policy.[2] The relationship between the civil and military structures was so close that the British War Cabinet often referred to 'EAM-ELAS' as if it were a single thing.

Pat's arrival coincided with a three-day Party pan-Macedonian meeting, attended by 'several thousand' resistance fighters, to cement the reorganization of ELAS from a federation of resistance groups into structured military units. From this moment, ELAS presented itself not as a guerrilla band but as a regular force, operating on army lines with army tactics.[3] The change looked like a preparation for a post-war power grab. ELAS Ninth Division took for itself the name of the Ninth Division of the regular army, which had beaten the Italians in 1942 on Mount Pindus. ELAS Ninth Division brought together the various left-wing armed bands in Western Macedonia, with men (and later women) from the Greek-speaking Aliakmon basin, the Grammos highlands further west towards Albania, and the mainly Slav-speaking villages to the north.

The SOE had established the Military Mission to develop and support resistance, to help liberate Greece from the Nazis, and generally to make life difficult for the Germans; the more German soldiers and equipment that could be kept in the Greek mountains, the better for the Allied campaigns elsewhere. The mission's staff was made up of a handful of SOE liaison officers, supported by NCO demolition specialists and wireless operators, with an assortment of Greek military personnel (who had returned at great personal risk). The SOE officers and men wore battledress, which was well adapted to fighting in the harsh conditions of the Greek mountains, was good for morale and – in theory – entitled them to be treated as prisoners of war should they fall into the hands of the enemy. In reality, it was no protection: Hitler's notorious 'commando orders', issued secretly in 1942, decreed that captured Allied commandos should be killed without trial, whether they were wearing proper uniforms or not. SOE personnel captured in Greece were liable to be tortured and shot, either on the spot or back in Germany.

The mission in Western Macedonia was numerically tiny: it could only operate by equipping and training local guerrillas and carrying out sabotage operations with them. It also had to follow the policies set by the War Cabinet in London and HQ Middle East in Cairo. Gold sovereigns were sent by Cairo and dropped in containers on the mountains above Pendalofos. Gold flowed through the mission to finance the resistance fighters – the *Andartes* – to pay for winter housing and to buy food for refugees whose villages had been burned. British gold entered the mythology of northern Greece. The mission's sardonic code-name for the Pendalofos station and radio was Boodle, 'ill-gotten gains'.

Almost the first thing Pat did on arriving in Pendalofos was to finish the letter he had started before leaving Cairo:

> Darling it's absolutely impossible. It's after 3 am and I simply can't answer your letters. Take it as written, will you, and forgive me. I have a long day ahead. There is too much to say and no time to say it in. A very merry Christmas. Sorry I can't send you anything. And a happy New Year. We'll have a long procession of very happy ones as long as we are together. Wait as patiently as you can. I love you, you're marvellous. Goodnight, my darling Jill. Your Pat.

Christmas was a long way off and no letters from Pat would reach England before the middle of the following February. Letters and parcels came in to the mission with the weapons and supplies flown over from Cairo, but there was no regular or reliable way to send mail back home.

Pat's first job, two weeks after dropping in Greece, was to hold a Commando and Demolitions course for ELAS fighters in the village of Vithos, which clings to the opposite mountainside, facing Pendalofos across a steep and picturesque gorge. The *Andartes* were extremely keen but lacked discipline and 'their officers were appalling.' The course culminated in a scheme to seize and demolish a guarded bridge by night. On his return to Pendalofos Pat found a 'terrific bunch of letters all at once – thirteen in all' from Jill but had little time to enjoy them. Almost immediately he set off again, to lay mines along the road running northward up the Aliakmon towards Albania, with orders that gave him a free hand to carry out any operations against the Germans he thought fit.

Each sheet of the beautiful 1:100,000 War Office maps of Greece, produced by the Geographical Section of the General Staff in 1944, covers an area of over 2,000 square kilometres. Sheet E4 'Kónitsa' shows the north Pindus Mountains from a line 20 kilometres south of Pendalofos all the way up to the Albanian border and the headwaters of the Aliakmon. In the whole area, there was no settlement larger than a village, hardly a metalled road and very few cart tracks.

The closest road to Pendalofos ended at a village called Morfi, 6 kilometres to the west. To the north and east, where the contours on the map cluster tightly together, monasteries and villages were strung like beads along the dotted red strings of mule tracks. The peaks, ridges and steep-cut valleys offered ideal terrain for guerrilla operations: small, mobile bands could descend from the heights to harass conventional forces on the supply routes in the valleys below.

Pat set out with Bombardier Kite, four Poles, two Czechs and a Frenchman, aiming for an area about 30 kilometres north of Pendalofos at a crossroads on the River Aliakmon. They travelled on foot, along the mule paths and tracks, keeping to the high ground. On the outward journey, the group's arrival near the village of Dragaisa, about halfway, coincided with a German sortie from Argos Orestikon to burn villages to the south of the town of Kastoria. The next day, Pat and his companions had to watch from the high ground as a German column of 600 or 700 men burned three more villages. Even though the walls were built of stone, the picturesque traditional houses were horribly vulnerable to fire, being constructed with horizontal wooden poles set into the walls to support the beams. When the wood burned, everything collapsed.

'There was no real fighting: the only opposition was machine gun fire at 1,500 metres and over, too far away to have any effect. The *Andarte* tactics were to sit safely on distant ridges,' Pat wrote. The Poles in Pat's party, who had escaped from German forces, said that the Germans would have withdrawn if just one company of *Andartes* had counter-attacked. In the afternoon, the Germans withdrew to their bases, burning another village on the way. Their objective was to contain the *Andartes* and keep them pushed back from the line of communication. On this occasion, 'the *Andartes* fought little and badly. It was a pathetic sight; a walkover for the Germans.'

Pat and his men returned to base disappointed and frustrated, having accomplished nothing. At the request of the *Andartes*, they had laid some mines and taken them up again; following *Andarte* intelligence, they had spent a night in an ambush on the road running south-west from the little town of Argos Orestikon, waiting for a German column that never came.

Pat brought back a distrust of *Andarte* information and their ability as a fighting force. The burned villages were on the front line of ELAS 1st Battalion, 28th Regiment; if ELAS fighters were unwilling to defend their home territory, how much less effective would they be in attacking the Germans? The regimental commander said that the German-led force had been 600 or 700 strong, including about 400 Italians, some *Komitadji* and EKKA personnel. *Komitadji* were armed militias set up by the occupiers, building on the resentment of Slav-speaking villages that had been badly treated by the Greek dictator Metaxas; they supported the Axis in the hope of escaping Greek dominance. EKKA ('National and Social Liberation') was a small resistance organization, which ELAS saw as a potential rival and would later eliminate; EKKA did not operate this far north and Pat did not believe the story of their presence. The ELAS commander attributed the German success to their greater mobility; Pat thought it was the result of *Andarte* unwillingness to engage the Germans at close quarters and a failure to understand the principles of guerrilla warfare:

> Always attack, never defend. Fight in small independent units, loosely unified by a general plan, but tactically independent and entirely self-contained; do not fight in large units closely articulated with each other, like a regular army. Do not like a regular army think in terms of a front; there is no front; the front is everywhere and nowhere. Be to the enemy what a disease is to a body: pervade his whole system, like microbes, damage it and throw it out of gear.[4]

ELAS was now trying to fight like a regular force and hold a fixed defence line on the higher foothills, above the rolling ground of the valley itself but below the mountains. The *Andartes* set up positions with trenches, dugouts with heavy roofs of earth and timber to withstand mortar bombs and artillery shells, and even a few field telephones. However, this meant taking the enemy on at his own game but without either the training or heavy weapons needed to hold a line. Pat thought that the British Special Forces should form bands of their own, which could fight either independently of the *Andartes* or in conjunction with them. This would give the mission a reliable force to carry out orders from Cairo, and would stimulate the *Andartes* to greater efforts by the spirit of emulation. Fresh supplies of arms should be made to depend on results.

Pat met his commanding officer for the first time on 11 October when Lieutenant Colonel Nick Hammond arrived back in Pendalofos after a sabotage operation and tactical conference in Central Macedonia. Hammond had been a classics don at Cambridge before the war; he had been making an archaeological survey of north-west Greece and southern Albania since 1930, and spoke fluent Greek and some Albanian. He had been recruited by the SOE back in 1941 and as an instructor at Haifa had earned the nickname 'Captain Guncotton'. In February 1943, Hammond was parachuted into Greece to carry out sabotage and develop operations with the Resistance. He wore a tremendous moustache, and was known to everyone as 'Eggs' (Hammond – ham and eggs – Eggs).

Pat suggested that the Poles, Czechs and the Frenchman would make the nucleus of an effective commando force; deserters from non-German units in the

German army, the Poles in particular, would swell the numbers. Eggs expressed no opinion on Pat's estimate of ELAS as a military force but agreed to give the plan a try. Pat could set out straight away to reconnoitre the routes to Albania from Kastoria and Nestorio. He could attack the enemy anywhere north of the Aliakmon, make whatever military mischief he could in the mountains, and try to contact the SOE Mission in Albania. He could take the same force as on his first sortie, with the addition of a Greek regular officer, Lieutenant Zotos. Zotos had dropped back into Greece the month before Pat and had now just returned from Albania, where he had been arrested by communist partisans as a nationalist spy; he had been fortunate to escape with his life.

This was the kind of thing Pat had come to Greece to do, but first he had to get arms for his commando. The *Andartes* took charge of all supplies from the moment the containers touched the ground at the drop zone, and only passed on things that were specifically marked for the mission. ELAS now did everything it could to withhold the weapons without refusing outright. British persistence won in the end.

Zotos and Pat left the main group at the little village of Ailias and went ahead alone to the larger village of Nestorio, on the Aliakmon, to get information about enemy dispositions. In the middle of the day, sporadic fighting broke out around the river crossing. At three in the afternoon, thirty Germans formed up behind an armoured car and went in to Lower Nestorio unopposed to burn the remaining houses. Two companies of *Andartes* ran away as the Germans approached. A single German infantry section 'moved about the landscape at their leisure, taking an *Andarte* machine-gun nest in their stride, and looking rather as if they were out for a walk'. When they had finished, the Germans rejoined the main body several kilometres away and returned to their base in Kastoria. Pat reported that the officer commanding ELAS First Battalion was competent and aggressive but his subalterns, NCOs and men did not obey orders or hold their ground. If the *Andartes* showed real fight, the Germans would be confined to the towns and main roads, but nothing could be done until the *Andartes* learned discipline under fire.

The next day, 19 October, Hammond telephoned: civil war had broken out and everyone must return at once to Pendalofos. Pat called his party at Ailias; they fixed a rendezvous and travelled back together. Nothing had been achieved and the plan to form guerrilla bands was stillborn.

Trouble had been brewing since the collapse of Italy on 8 September. There were only a few Italian soldiers in Western Macedonia, based in Kastoria, but in Thessaly to the south there were 15,000 men of the Pinerolo Division with all their arms and equipment. What would they do? Whose side would they be on?

Following the surrender, the Italians agreed to come over to the Allied Military Mission and fight the Germans alongside the Greek resistance. They would not, however, collaborate with ELAS, who they thoroughly distrusted. ELAS did not have the resources to hold and feed a whole division in one region, so 4,000 Italians were escorted north into Western Macedonia, in the wet and chilly autumn weather. At a halt in the little town of Grevena, an ELAS commander delivered a speech to this miserable group, suggesting they should give up the idea of fighting the Germans in the mountains and simply hand over their arms. In return, ELAS would provide them with the same rations as the *Andartes*. The speech was eloquent and the choice was simple. All 4,000 Italians laid down their weapons and, in the cold rain, marched away to make camp at a village called Dotsiko.

ELAS was now better armed and much less dependent on the British for weapons, but it still wanted money. In mid-October, on orders from Cairo, 18,000 sovereigns were handed over to the Ninth Division as support for 6,000 *Andartes*. ELAS now had both arms and gold. Three days later, it launched a series of attacks on its right-wing rival resistance movement, EDES.

The Germans in turn took advantage of the conflict to attack both ELAS and EDES in a major drive, by two mountain divisions, against the main left-wing and right-wing resistance groups. On 20 to 21 October, powerful German forces approached Pendalofos in a pincer movement from the north-east and the west. ELAS Ninth Division melted away into the mountains. Hammond ordered the mission staff to move, with their stores, westward into the mountains by mule-track to the village of Eptachori 15 kilometres away. This little group, about a platoon in strength, had few weapons and little winter clothing. Pat was sent up to the high ground above Eptachori to receive an emergency drop of supplies. On three successive nights, the plane circled over the target but was unable to make the drop because of bad weather. After four or five days, the Germans gave up chasing shadows, the threat receded and everyone returned to base.

Liaison officers' laconic reports give no idea of the difficulties of dropping and receiving stores, weapons and explosives in the mountains. Almost everything was delivered in metal cylinders 35 x 175 centimetres, weighing up to 100 kilograms, with four carrying handles. Packing them with weapons, explosives, gold, clothes, cigarettes and emergency rations, filling every cranny in such a way that nothing broke or exploded when the container hit the ground, was a slow, painstaking business. Fragile radio sets had to be heavily padded with kapok wadding. Boots and clothing, on the other hand, need not go in a container but could be parcelled up and thrown out of the plane. Organizing a drop was a complex logistical operation. Every container had to be labelled and loaded onto the right plane. Exact locations and target times had to be agreed between headquarters, the liaison officers on the ground and the RAF, whose navigators had to work out the route, with alternatives in case of the unexpected. At the drop site, the 'reception committee' marked out the target area with three lights (occasionally fires in very remote areas, where burn marks would not be noticed) and flashed a code signal with a lamp to the aircraft circling overhead. Each container was released from the bomb bay on a line that first pulled open the parachute and then broke under the container's weight. On the ground, weapons, explosives, radio sets and gold sovereigns were loaded onto mules and carried back to base over tracks through the mountains, avoiding anything in the nature of a road.

The drop zone for Pendalofos was at a place called Paliokrimini, a good 12 kilometres away from Boodle as the crow flies, where the mountains rise to 1,800 metres. An open patch of ground on the ridge below the summit, surrounded by trees and miles away from any road, made this a good, safe place. Pat's diaries and notes mention walking to and from the drop zone and encounters with *Andartes* on the way, but give no idea of the remoteness of the place or the harshness of the terrain. In the summer, when the air on the bare mountainside is warm and sweet with the scent of herbs and the woods are loud with birdsong, Paliokrimini would be a strenuous but enjoyable hike. In the winter, when the tracks were treacherous with mud and snow, the task of fetching supplies, gold, weapons and explosives down from the mountaintop was arduous in the extreme.

Pat and his small party of helpers must have waited first in the woods and then on the bare mountain ridge in foul weather, probably snow, while the plane circled, unable to make the drop. Then they would have had to trudge wearily back down to Eptachori to repeat the attempt the night after and again the one after that.

In response to the outbreak of civil war, on 31 October the BBC broadcast a statement that ELAS was guilty of starting the conflict and GHQ Middle East stopped all relief and payments to them. In retaliation, the Ninth Division placed the mission staff under village arrest: none of them could leave Pendalofos, for any reason, without a special permit and an ELAS escort.

The mission was billeted in a substantial stone house, built on the side of the slope and reached by a steep lane from the central village square. Steps led from the lane down to a little gatehouse with a path to a side entrance. On the uphill side, the house was two-storeyed; on the opposite face, the ground fell away and there was a substantial storage cellar. The house fronted onto a garden with a terrace, overlooked by a first-floor balcony from which Eggs addressed the crowds. ELAS put a guard on the house, allegedly to protect the British against the anger of villagers. There were several demonstrations, one of which was decidedly hostile, and innumerable deputations. Hammond, Captain Prentice, Pat, Kite, the RAF radio operator Leo Voller and several newly-arrived NCOs, together with two Greek officers, settled down to a period of confinement, wrangling, anxiety and frustration.

Civil war in northern Greece caused consternation in the War Cabinet in London, with repercussions that reached as far as Moscow and Washington. Rex

Leeper, the British Ambassador to the Greek government-in-exile in Cairo, fired off a telegram to Churchill. Leeper had been Head of the Foreign Office Political Intelligence Department and a member of the Political Warfare Executive; the prime minister and foreign secretary listened to him very carefully. Churchill reacted with a volcanic memo to the Foreign Office and Lord Selborne:

> Reference Tel. No. 335 from H.M. Ambassador to the Greek Government. EAM and ELAS should be starved and struck at by every means in our power. But I fear these means are small. Pray let me have proposals. We must know which side we are on. There is still time to communicate with the F[oreign] S[ecretary] in Cairo. W.S.C. 3.XI.

Lord Selborne, Minister for Economic Warfare who had direct responsibility for the SOE, replied in detail the next day. Churchill's suggestions were not practicable, he wrote: Greeks regarded the defeat of the Germans as inevitable and believed the political party in power at the time of an armistice would form the government. EAM (whose policy, of course, was directed by the communists) felt it should seize power now. The only card in the British hand was an offer to supervise post-war elections, so that they would be fair. It was impossible to take an openly anti-ELAS stand for several reasons, the first being that there were about eighty British personnel with ELAS units. The SOE officers, their radio operators and NCO demolitions experts were effectively hostages. Bombing ELAS was unthinkable and cutting off supplies would not be much of a deterrent, now they had the equipment from the surrendered Italians. Any declaration of war on ELAS would result in the murder of the British liaison officers and achieve nothing positive. However much the British distrusted the left-wing ELAS, the right-wing EDES was no substitute as a national resistance movement. Britain had very few options: the only practical course was to call on the Greeks to stop fighting each other; to guarantee a free post-war plebiscite supervised by British police; and to send a very senior British officer to try to persuade the Greeks – left and right alike – to reorganize the guerrilla bands into a new National Army of Liberation. The king of the Hellenes should be advised to announce that he would devote his energies to re-victualling Greece and would not return to the country until after post-war elections. Britain had underestimated the king's unpopularity, which arose from his association with the pre-war dictatorship of Ioannis Metaxas; the government had not used the BBC or propaganda to build up the king, and had provoked and enraged the ELAS leaders by inviting them to talks in Cairo and then sending them back empty-handed.

Ten days later, on 14 November 1943, Foreign Secretary Anthony Eden presented the War Cabinet with a more political view.[5] Britain should honour her alliance with the king and the government-in-exile to ensure that the country did not fall into chaos or dictatorship after the war, and strengthen relations between the countries to support British strategic positions in south-east Europe and the Mediterranean. A post-war EAM regime would be a communist dictatorship, which would look to Russia, not England (although the Russians showed no interest in Greece and accepted it as part of the British sphere of interest). ELAS bands had little or no military use against the Germans; their main value was to provide 'safe harbourage for the British officers who themselves carry out all the sabotage'. However, given the unpopularity of the king, the monarchy could not survive unless EAM's influence was broken. Britain should end relations with EAM-ELAS; the king should declare that he would set up a Regency Council as soon as Greece was liberated and not return until after elections. The king should also secretly authorize the archbishop of Athens to make the necessary arrangements and encourage him to develop moderate opinion. 'We may hope,' Eden concluded, that following a break with ELAS any loss of 'facilities' for British officers in ELAS-controlled areas would be only temporary and that other nationalist bands might appear to provide the necessary 'safe harbourage' from the Germans.

Where Selborne had been blunt, Eden was airy. He agreed that ELAS was a murderous gang bent on taking over the country, and that EDES – the next largest grouping – was no match for it in size or power, but did not suggest how alternative nationalist bands might appear or how they might survive against either ELAS or the SS Mountain Divisions. He did not address the probability that ELAS would simply murder the SOE officers and men.

Back in Pendalofos, the liaison officers passed the time as best they could, organizing card games and *tavli* competitions (the Greek version of backgammon), and making friends with the village children. The *psevdhaetos* or 'false eagle', made of a paper cone like a big dunce's hat with a candle end or taper on a light frame of wood at the bottom, was a particular hit. With luck and a perfectly calm day, when the candle was lit and the hot air rose, the whole contraption would float entrancingly up into the sky.[6]

Pat observed the political manoeuvres of ELAS Ninth Division, improved his Greek, had silk shirts, underwear and pyjamas made from his parachute, and wrote his diary.[7]

31 October 1943

It was a pleasant sedate day – a Sunday. I had a late breakfast, about 9 am. Fried eggs and coffee and marmalade and coarse brown bread as usual, a perfect start to any day. I read or wrote or talked during the morning. At 4 o'clock (the appointment was for 3.30) I went over to Apostolos's house

and he and Mrs Lambrinisis and I went with a bundle of parachute silk
and cords to the house of a dressmaker in Vithos. On the way, near the
Stratigio [EAM/ELAS HQ], we met Stavros the journalist, the Bishop
of Kozani's secretary in a grey raincoat, with no hat and a two-day's stub-
ble like silver filings. He saluted me in his dreadful French.

For part of the way we were accompanied by a young middle-aged
widow dressed in black, a friend of Apostolos and his wife. She was
now a refugee from a village about eight hours journey away, which had
been burnt. She and a number of others had come to ask Karatsas [the
kapetanios of ELAS Ninth Division] for relief. He is pure fox: he gives
when it suits his own interests and those of his party and if it doesn't
suit he refuses with perfect callousness, however smoothly he may show
sympathy or distress. Apostolos and his wife pressed the woman to
stay the night at their house but she refused. On both sides there was
that peculiar mixture of real feeling with ulterior calculation that is so
characteristic of the Greeks. There was evidently more than met the eye
in this matter of a simple invitation; few matters are simple in Greece.

It was a peaceful, clear autumn afternoon with a cold pale blue sky in
which were shelves of cloud like the grey, lemon and smoke brown shelves
of rock strata on the hillsides. The autumn trees were very beautiful –
tall poplars with trunks like mercury and leaves still bright sap green,
gnarled and frizzly chestnut trees dropping their nuts, beeches orange
and yellow, and one or two sycamores like red candles at Christmas –
all these clustered round Vithos. While Apostolos's wife tripped ahead
through the mud and stones of the mountain path in her high-heeled
shoes, Apostolos and I, as befits men in the Balkan idea, walked in a
dignified and leisurely manner behind, engaged in deep converse.

Vithos, in those days, was a village of tailors, with a large fabric store on the far side
of the village above the local EAM offices in a building that is now the village café.

The tailor's house was a large, tall square one (large by local standards,
by ours little more than a cottage) in the lower half of the village. It was
of stone, as was the roof, and there was the inevitable balcony. We saw the
dressmaker, her mother, and her grandmother. The first was a fine young
woman of about twenty-five, big-hipped and high-busted but light in
her movements. She had absolutely black hair, the curious secret beauty
about the eyes and eyelids which is typical of Greek beauty though so few
have it – a look of having just spent a night with her lover and of having
risen refreshed, a look of having secrets she would tell no-one, not even

to him, downcast eyes and the slightest smile curling the corners of the lips. Actually she was rather a simple stupid creature with good looks and manners. She had a ring on her finger, presumably from an absent husband, and I am sure hadn't a lover. She was the superior, modern member of the family; she wore European clothes of her own making and her dressmaker's diploma and the picture of a Haussmann-style building in a city hung on the wall.

Of course, there was no chance of getting down to business at once. We had to sit eating chestnuts and walnuts and talking about nothing, which irritated me. I amused myself by looking round the room, which was excellently planned and finished in the traditional style. There was a wide, open fireplace with logs on end and a single egg being hard-boiled. The wall opposite the fireplace consisted entirely of wooden cupboards, which made the room seem cosy and so did the ceiling, which was made completely of nicely tailored wood. On either side of the fireplace was a window, one of which had a bunch of basil tied up in a top corner. Flanking the hearth and extending toward the middle of the room were two double beds covered with thick peasant blankets woven in stripes of various dark, warm colours. In front of the hearth was a cat rolled up in a ball, breathing peacefully. The only flaws were the lack of any pictures or evidence of music, with not even a guitar hanging on the wall.

Her mother was a sodden, bending creature dressed in far too many clothes (of the peasant style); she had a face like creased yellow oilskin, steel spectacles, damp wispy hair of indefinable colour, and a fund of wailing nonsense about everything and nothing. She had more than kept up with the Joneses all her life. It turned out that the gentle-voiced, cultured theological student whom I had met in the days of our Commando course at Vithos was, like the dressmaker, the child of this female Jeremiah. And that he is a very undutiful child and never goes to see his mother – for which I don't blame him. Apostolos said he had read that you could always tell whether a man was good or not by whether he loved his mother. Afterwards he told me 'that man is one of my best, my greatest friends. I always reverenced him very much for his learning.' This bit of pious and innocent treachery is the sort of thing which Apostolos, for all his intelligence and good nature, lets slip by him now and again.

After quarter of an hour, the grandmother came in, one of those fine old peasant women who combine the sympathies of a democrat with the courtesy which is noticeable in a few English aristocrats. I could have talked to her for hours.

But the moment came for negotiation. Apostolos and his wife wanted to get home in time for tea. The dressmaker, he and I retired to the landing. He parlayed on my behalf and I weakly agreed to the outrageous price of 300,000 drachmas (about a guinea in paper money) for six shirts, four pairs of pyjamas and a silk scarf. Apostolos, that lamb of innocence, then asked the dressmaker in an undertone whether he must pay at the same rate for the single shirt he is having made for himself, out of a piece of parachute I have given him.

It was dusk when we set out again for their home and there was a nip in the air. Apostolos said to his wife: 'Go ahead of us to prepare the tea' and she flew away up the stiff climb over the rocks. I drank my tea with the Colonel and Leo and after thanking the Lambrinises returned here, to make the graceful descent through the evening, dinner and a book to the clean white bed in which I sleep so well and comfortably. Sleep is certainly a gift of God. One can use no other expression, even if there is no God.

Two weeks later, Pat wrote to Jill: 'Just by way of making you jealous, let me tell you that I have invested in a number of silk shirts and silk pyjamas. They're marvellous and the pyjamas surprise me by being very warm to sleep in.' It was, of course, impossible to post the letter. To reassure Jill, Pat arranged for a series of cables to be sent from headquarters in Cairo, saying: 'From Lt Evans to codename Cottage quote safe as houses letters great pleasure love Pat unquote.'

There was a darker side to life in Pendalofos. On 1 November, two raggedly-dressed Yugoslav officers asked to be taken in by the mission. Otherwise, they would be sent to Tito by way of Albania and either on the way or on arrival they would be shot. Beating was a common method both of obtaining evidence and of changing people's opinions:

> The schoolmaster of Vithos used to speak to all and sundry against communism and against EAM/ELAS. He was thrown into jug and beaten up and became zealous for communism, so much so that I am told he is likely to be bumped off when the other side gets in again.

When a local man escaped from the prison some months earlier, his wife was arrested and beaten up; she gave away her husband's hiding place and he was caught. Vigorous *Andarte* singing could often be heard from the direction of the ELAS prison, sometimes in harmony, with girls' voices as well as men's, one song following another with hardly a pause for breath. The Greek officers attached to the mission said the singing was meant to drown the cries of people being beaten.

ELAS's execution ground was further away, in a secluded, wooded spot, chosen so that the sound of shots would not carry to the mission in the village.

EAM/ELAS was ruthless in hunting down and intimidating any potential opposition:

> …it was about 2 November that four people were brought from Avyerinos and imprisoned here. These are the priest, his son, the eldest Guinis and another man said to be a telegraph operator. The common rumour is that they are accused of 'opposing the struggle'. As far as I know they have not yet been tried. A villager said they would probably be sentenced to a term of imprisonment, which would also entail their being beaten a lot with a view to changing their political opinions.

Philippos, the eldest Guinis, had left Avyerinos for America, where he had run a restaurant with his brother in the 1920s. The business had been a success; Philippos had returned home wealthy to invest in property in Macedonia's great city, Thessaloniki (or Salonika as it was then known) and become the headman of his native village. The Germans had requisitioned his town house and he had moved back to Avyerinos, where Pat had stayed a night on the way back from Nestorio to Pendalofos in October. Far from being an ELASite, Philippos was a nationalist, who supported the right; he was fortunate to survive to write in praise of Pat in 1946.

The EAM/ELAS command, the *Stratigio*, was doing everything they dared to annoy and obstruct the British, short of imprisoning them. Throughout November and early December, there was a battle of wills between the *Stratigio* and the mission. As Pat noted in his diary on 9 November:

> The political officers of the *Stratigio* know quite well what they would like to do but they cannot decide what they will do. Their line of action will depend on the train of events in larger spheres, on our own firmness and patience in maintaining our line as laid down by Cairo, on our own refusal to get rattled, and on their own temperaments, which are unstable and combustible. A sudden break of fortune, good or bad, or a weak step or a high-handed move by us, might infuriate or encourage them into some form of violence or insult against us. For my part I believe that although there may be minor insults or hostile demonstrations, nothing particular will befall us. The organization is in a weak position and knows it.

EAM and ELAS were under political pressure from two sides: from the British, who had the money, and from the people, who were suffering a good deal from the occupation, and from German reprisals for resistance activities. As the weather worsened, snow began to fall and the Germans continued to burn villages; the need for relief grew urgent. While the British were keen to provide aid to the villagers, they were determined not to let EAM/ELAS get their hands on any more gold. There was also the question of what would become of the Italians if ELAS reneged on its promise to feed them.

Throughout November, the mission, Cairo and ELAS argued and wrangled about terms. Cairo was prepared to provide relief to destitute refugees, but ELAS must not handle funds at any time.[8] Relief should be provided in kind, by soup kitchens supervised by Allied Military Mission personnel, as a humanitarian policy for genuinely extreme cases; support to ELAS was in abeyance until the civil war ended. ELAS Ninth Division rejected Cairo's terms. Pat thought this was natural: accepting the conditions would be to lose face in a region where they had enjoyed almost absolute power. The mission, though, was confident that ELAS would give way in the end, and the longer they resisted, the more political support they would lose.

On 15 November, Boodle told Cairo that there were not enough British officers to handle all the money and supplies, and suggested that reliable Greeks might be chosen to assist in staffing the dropping ground, buying and distributing supplies and providing medical services. A week later, Cairo confirmed that compensation payments for houses burned by the Germans were now banned; any money handled by Greeks in ELAS areas was sure to find its way to EAM/ELAS, so some method had to be found of administering relief that did not involve ELAS. Could this be done through village committees or church dignitaries? Would it be possible for village priests to issue relief through soup kitchens or with the help of village food committees under their control?

Boodle pointed out that EAM controlled the village organizations and British liaison officers could not buy food in bulk in enemy-controlled areas without risk of ELAS interference. ELAS would not, however, rob or hinder the peasants, who would be able to buy food themselves. Hammond proposed that village committees consisting of the priest, the schoolmaster and the *proedros* (the elected headman) should compile lists of people in need of relief; a liaison officer should check the lists and pay money for one month to those in need. A church dignitary and a civilian doctor would, if possible, accompany him on his tour.

Villagers had been coming to Pendalofos to petition the mission since the beginning of November. They came as People's Committees, ranging from two to thirty men, on foot from as far as the town of Grevena, a walk of some 40 kilometres. Many of the men had very bad shoes; few of them had waterproofs to protect them from the autumn rain and fog. Sometimes several deputations came and presented their case together; otherwise they queued up outside, bedraggled and miserable, to wait their turn.[9] Most of the deputations included one or two committed EAM/

ELAS enthusiasts, who argued passionately. Many of the petitioners, though, were simple villagers with no political conviction beyond a love of their country and a desire for the war to end. They were usually very cordial to the English, although they sometimes hesitated to show it. The deputation often contained a priest or two and one or two of the better-educated, more prosperous people.

Each deputation brought a round-robin letter, signed by all its members, condemning the broadcast by 'the wireless station of London' that had blamed ELAS for starting the civil war. The petition demanded that an Allied committee of inquiry, with British, American, Russian and Greek representatives, should be set up 'to determine the truth', and that London should broadcast the results. The distribution list included three ELAS Divisional Headquarters, the overall ELAS HQ, the Joint Allied HQ, the British, American and Russian governments and, on at least one occasion, the government of China.

Hammond let the deputations talk. When they started shouting, he kept his voice at a conversational level; if he started a sentence, he always continued and finished it, no matter how often he was swamped by the rising tide of interruption. An Allied Committee of Inquiry had already determined the truth: its findings were those broadcast by the BBC. He would ask: 'Do you believe the radio station of London when it says the Russians have advanced?' 'Yes,' would come the answer. 'Do you believe it when it says the Allies have captured Sicily, or are approaching Rome?' 'Yes.' 'Then why don't you believe it when it says ELAS has attacked EDES?'

The deputations often wanted to know whether there were any Russian officers in Greece and, if so, whether they took part in the committee of inquiry. On being told 'No', they asked 'Why?' Eggs replied that he hoped the Russians would send some officers soon but that so far only British, Americans and Greeks had been attached to the mission because the Russians had no troops in Greece or the Middle East.

Hammond soon noticed that most of the round robins were written on the same kind of paper and many of the declarations were in the same handwriting. The deputations of civilians, often from villages where they were staying as refugees after their own had been burned, were more interested in knowing when they were going to start getting sovereigns, blankets, food and medicines. A friendly, impoverished little group, who arrived tired and wet from some distant village, finally let the truth out of the bag. They did not say anything about the broadcast but simply begged for help. Hammond told them that the British were anxious to resume help at once, on the most liberal scale, but ELAS would not agree conditions. The British would resume civilian relief immediately ELAS agreed, but could not give any military help until the civil war had stopped and it was sure that the arms and equipment would be used to kill Germans, not Greeks. As they were preparing to leave, having talked of nothing but their own plight and need, Eggs asked if they knew anything about the BBC broadcast. 'Oh,' they exclaimed, rather sheepishly, 'we don't really want to discuss it. This [taking out a round robin] was given us when we arrived and we were told to hand it to you and make a protest in line with what it says.' They shook hands and left. Another deputation, consisting of two old gentlemen and one priest, were so struck by Hammond's good sense that they exclaimed: 'We should be addressing ourselves not to you but to our own *Stratigio*: it is they who are holding things up.'

ELAS intended to put so much pressure on the mission that Hammond would cave in and ask Cairo to repudiate the broadcast statement. However, the result had been the opposite: by sending the village committees to Pendalofos, the *Stratigio* gave the British the means to tell the people that it was ELAS, not EDES, who had started the civil war and was now preventing relief. ELAS still held on to popular support, having gained a strong grip by a combination of terrorism, propaganda and some real military and administrative achievements. However, the point about relief struck home; word got round that the British were ready to help.

ELAS had underestimated the British. One of the Greek officers attached to the mission remarked to Pat: 'Before I came out from Greece to the Middle East I thought the English were weak and soft, easily cajoled or coerced. Since then I have found just the opposite. I have realized that if the English say "No" nothing in heaven or earth will move them.'

ELAS's military commander in Macedonia, Demaratos (who had been a regular colonel in the Greek army Ninth Division) was impatient to get on with the war and resented the intrusion of civilian politicians. Pat believed that the *kapetanios* 'wily, unscrupulous and resourceful Karatsas' and senior EAM representatives were responsible for the time-wasting psychological tactics and gave vent to his frustration in his notebook:

ELAS is an inefficient military organization and a political body bent on securing absolute power in Greece after the war, or earlier if possible; caring little at heart for the plight of the people or for winning the war except as these affect their political chances; willing to see villages burn undefended in order that the troops shall be kept intact for war against political opponents instead of against the Germans, now, and that the refugees by having to depend on them for food and shelter may willy-nilly become its adherents; beating up dissenters, or torturing them, in order to secure assent or evidence and when this fails, assassinating them, with or without the formality of a trial – methods which for being habitual in the Balkans do not arouse any the less anger and hatred; greedily accepting the gold sovereigns of the British but using them for propaganda and for amassing small private fortunes, and spending only as much as is politically profitable on the real object of the help, namely materials for resisting the enemy and relieving those who have suffered from the enemy; behaving towards the British sometimes as fawning flatterers and sometimes like the monkey which knows enough to grab what you offer it but not enough to say thank you; conducting a whispering campaign against the British, on whom the country depends for food, supplies and other essentials, doing all they can to lower Great Britain in the eyes of the people and to obstruct the members of the Mission in their daily work; idolizing Russia and the Soviet system, which well over 50% of the people do not want, both because the Greeks are by nature the least Communistic of all Europeans and because it is felt that the protective Russian aegis, after the 'Red October' as before, will be only the grasp of a pan-Slav octopus. The movement which started out in the colours of a nation rising up to defend its soil against a harsh and rapacious invader, and which was far more determined and better organized than any other movement with the same aim in Greece, and therefore spread much more rapidly, has gradually come out in its real form: that of a vehicle for a few worthless but astute politicians. The minor officials, such as the political officers of Divisions and below, the fighting officers, the members of the civilian administration and relief bodies and of the youth organization, are either honest dupes or willing tools; mostly the former. That is to say, they honestly believe, or think they believe, in communism, though hardly any of them know, even as a matter of textbook definition, what communism is, and it is certain that most of these pathetic and rather likeable enthusiasts would conceive a strong distaste for communism if they understood it or if it were introduced. The Greek is an individualist, more than that an atomist. He hates combining even more than the British farmer does. *Due Grecchi, cinque capitani.* He is not a Communist. He would never stand, unless it were too strong for him to overthrow, the tyranny that Communism imposes in its early stages and perhaps in its later ones too (for the noble conception created by Marx and Engels is only a dream; a poem, but not a political system). So even in its epic, ideal form the system would never have suited Greece. As for the common ramp which is now masquerading here as the thing described in the great and optimistic Manifesto, and as an offshoot of the present epic of Russia, but which bears as little resemblance to its mask as a fifth rate actor to a character in Aeschylus, if those who believe the imposture genuine knew what it was, and if those who know what it is dared to speak and move, they would turn in a body and destroy it.

Winter was on the way and soon there would be thick snow. Pat wanted a pair of skis. One afternoon, he went to see the carpenter, who had a little workshop just beyond the end of the garden and was unhappy at being obliged to work for ELAS, making rifle stocks for a pittance. After some introductory talk and getting a knife sharpened, Pat broached the reason for his visit. They had trouble over the word 'ski' at first: there are two or three Greek words that sound practically the same; each had to be discussed in turn before Pat could explain what he really wanted. The carpenter said yes of course he knew, and drew a very inaccurate picture of a ski and its curves. 'It was all very leisurely and great fun.' Making a pair of skis would be easy, the carpenter said, when he had a few days off. He would use a tough, springy kind of wood, which was normally used for making wooden barrels. He would bend the planks by heating them near a fire and setting the shape on a former. The next day, 23 November, Pat wrote to Jill:

> I am having an unexpectedly slack time and amusing myself with a language and some reading and some writing. Of course there is the usual hush-hush about my movements and actions (though at the moment they are nil). I had lunch and climbed a hill to walk off the effects of a magnificent apple pie. A fine day, pure sunny air; it was a pleasant walk.

Change, as well as winter, was in the air. The civil war, and the resulting tension with the British, became too much for Colonel Demaratos, who resigned as military commander and withdrew to his village. His replacement as General of Ninth Division, Karayiannis, came to tea to meet Eggs. Pat did not take to Karayiannis on first meeting:

> He is a small, stumpy man with a long nose, a lined face, hair like the pile of a carpet, an air of resignation and a considerable docility towards ELAS. Altogether he is a disappointment: a firebrand or a man of action would have been preferable as our future collaborator, whereas this fellow seems to be nothing but a willing tool. But these are just first impressions and may be wrong.

Negotiations about relief were progressing. ELAS proposed that the refugees should elect village committees. Mission staff would be allowed free movement to deliver aid, provided they were accompanied by an ELAS guard and watched 'to prevent enemies of EAM and ELAS sowing dissension between the Allies and EAM/ELAS.'[10] ELAS wanted to exclude Pat, on the pretext that he had made propaganda for Zervas (the commander of ELAS's right-wing rival group EDES) in Avyerinos on the journey back from Nestorio.

'This was entirely untrue,' Pat wrote, 'Lt Col Hammond's immediate reply to the accusations was to say that a court of enquiry must be held. ELAS agreed, but said they must have a little time to get the documents of the case together – they said they had got signed statements of evidence, but these statements were not at Pendalofos. Naturally, they never could produce any evidence and the court of enquiry was never held.'[11]

ELAS proposed to restrict British presence at the dropping ground to one member of the mission, to control the entry of mission officers to areas near the enemy, and to prohibit them from carrying out relief activities beyond the Aliakmon. Hammond would not agree.

Genuine deputations from villages were now coming to plead for help, 'unable to grasp failure of Allies to force ELAS/EAM on relief'.[12] Their need was great: in Western Macedonia alone, hundreds of villages had been burned and tens of thousands of people displaced as the occupiers systematically tried to crush the Greek rebellion by reprisals against the civilian population.[13]

However, there was still no action. In a letter to Jill, Pat described his 30th birthday celebrations on 1 December 1943: 'We had an enormous lunch, with me sitting at one end of the table and another chap, whose birthday was a few days ago, at the other; we had three kinds of drink, and an enormous pie made of honey and walnuts.' Ten days later, presents arrived: 'Today has been a terrific day. I came over to breakfast to find all my mail and your two presents and a number of magazines and newspapers piled up on my plate.' The presents were books, a collection of cartoons from the *New Yorker* by Peter Arno, and *Les Yeux d'Elsa* by the French poet Louis Aragon; a third, the collected poems of Paul Verlaine, had gone missing in transit 'but will probably turn up later'.

Finally, on 18 December ELAS agreed to the resumption of relief on terms drawn up by Hammond:

1. In every village where are situated victims of arson, refugees by reason of enemy attack, families of war casualties, families of war hostages, and disabled people of the 1940–41 war, the priest, schoolmaster and *proedros* and two of the war victims, whom the war victims themselves shall elect freely and democratically, shall be members of the aid committee. If one of the first three is missing or does not enjoy the confidence of the war victims the war victims shall choose a deputy. This committee shall prepare lists of the war victims in need and shall examine the needs of each family.

2. Members of the AMM [Allied Military Mission] will visit each village and after examining the lists will give to the families assistance in person. I shall be grateful if the district doctors and the district priests assist the AMM. The HQ 9 Div is free to send both *Andartes* and the representatives of the HQ, who will advise the Mission on the representatives forming the committees in areas under German control.
3. The district doctors, or if they are missing the doctors conscripted into ELAS, will estimate the medical needs of the war victims and will report to AMM.
4. HQ 9 Div will give freedom of movement specifically for this work to the members of the Mission. When danger exists for the entry of AMM, the officer representative of HQ 9 Div on the spot and the officer of AMM on the spot will reach agreement as to how far they can proceed, or if they do not agree will not pass into the area under dispute but will make a report to their superior officers.
5. If the question is asked in the village 'Whence comes the aid?' the answer shall be 'Gift of the Allies'.
6. Where they cannot proceed, the AMM will call the committee of the village, or as many members of the committee as are able, to come to a centre. If the officer of AMM thinks fit, he will give the aid and the committee will be obliged to bring the nominal receipts.

Since the AMM has not the order to assist the destitute families of the *Andartes* as a separate category, the AMM promises to request GHQ Middle East to permit the assistance of these also.

The AMM promises to give the aid in accordance with the above conditions.

The HQ 9 Div promises to assist the AMM in this work in accordance with the above terms.

Agreed on 18.12.43 at Pendalofos by EGGS and by KARAYIANNIS (GOC 9 Div), having been written by EGGS and the translation made by him.[14]

The next day Hammond, Pat, Captain Prentice and Captain Backhouse (a new arrival, based in Eptachori) set out separately through the snow to deliver relief. Each was accompanied by an ELAS *Andarte* to see that they made no propaganda for the British.

The task was immense: by the time the four British officers returned to Pendalofos on Christmas Eve they had distributed some 4,000 gold sovereigns in relief aid to 250 villages to support 16,000 villagers at a rate of a quarter of a sovereign per head.[15]

Before aid resumed, Cairo warned Boodle that the scheme in Western Macedonia was just a pilot to see how the civilian population reacted and what resources were really needed. After the first distribution, HQ ELAS Ninth Division sent the village committees a circular, drafted by Hammond:

> The distribution is an experiment in West Macedonia alone. There is no certainty that it will occur again, and no probability that if it does occur again it will be expanded to include other categories. Continuation depends on the needs of the Allies and on the sincere cooperation of each committee and of each village.
>
> The duty of each committee, as it is responsible to the Allies, is to list only those who are starving, providing they belong to the stated category. For that reason the committee is obliged to examine strictly the needs of each category, because this aid is an aid against death.
>
> The duty of those who accept the gift is to buy foodstuffs at once. Gold is given only because we cannot give foodstuffs as the Red Cross does.
>
> The Western Macedonians should understand that this winter there will be greater danger of starvation than hitherto. All who can move to more well off areas, where the Red Cross is, should go. Those who stay in the mountain villages must help one another. The Allies care for you with their blood and when they give you a gift in time of war that gift is necessarily small and perhaps may not be enough to cover the needs of the various starving nations.

Mercifully the relief missions continued, although not all the officers on the ground were pleased. On New Year's Eve, station 'Mortlake' grumpily telegraphed Cairo from Mount Vermion: 'Touring burnt villages is no job for a sapper officer. Civil relief is important but do not turn AMM into Red Cross. Until you send properly qualified people to do it as a whole time job we are doing nothing but nibble at the problem and waste good officers.'

Those delivering relief had to walk immense distances through the snowy mountains, sleep in whatever shelter the villagers could provide and keep their wits about them. On a tour of villages between Pendalofos and Argos Orestikon, Pat came across what looked like a systematic attempt at fraud:

> In several villages my attention was caught by the large number of men presenting themselves with doctor's certificates to the effect that they

were disabled and incapable of any kind of work. These certificates were signed by Doctor X. On 10 January I called on Doctor X in village Z to discuss the category of the disabled, which he was interpreting much more widely than I under the terms of my order was able to do. During the course of the discussion he declared, without me having mentioned either directly or indirectly the subject of money, that he had taken no payment for any of the certificates he had made out. The next day at village Y several men told the Divisional Representative that the doctor had demanded payment from them for the certificate of disablement; and the commander of the Vitsi Battalion told me that several men had come to him with complaints of the same thing.

Events in Western Macedonia were exercising the policy-makers in London, Cairo and Moscow. The Foreign Office felt that it was worth sticking with the Greek resistance movement, if only for the sake of morale. Rex Leeper and the commander-in-chief in Cairo, General Alexander, had serious reservations. Just as aid was resuming, Leeper cabled London, arguing that ELAS's behaviour was undermining morale and even making the Germans seem preferable to the *Andartes*:

> Internecine strife, always latent among the Greeks, is now eclipsing hatred of the enemy…. The Commander-in-Chief rightly feels that his task is a military one. He has a limited supply of aircraft at his disposal for sending supplies and he wishes to use them to the best military advantage. Clearly the partisans of Yugoslavia should have them.[16]

The commander-in-chief also disliked British officers being 'involved increasingly in political wrangles or administering quite inadequate relief'. Leeper believed that the poor quality of the resistance leadership had rendered the task of British officers in Greece impossible. ELAS leaders had been 'thoroughly bad and unrepresentative of the real Greek sentiment', while the EDES commander, Zervas, had failed to capture the popular imagination. Leeper advised that the whole mess should be handed over to the Greek government-in-exile, since 'I do not believe that further Greek resistance under present conditions can help the war effort against the Germans, while it will certainly inflict uncalled for hardship on a people who, whatever their failings, have a warm affection for the British.' However, two days later on 21 December, Leeper telegraphed that both Zervas and the leadership of ELAS/EAM were ready to consider steps to end the civil war. The same day, the Greek prime minister in exile, Mr Tsouderos, broadcast an appeal for all resistance forces in Greece to stop fighting each other.

A government-in-exile has no citizens, no legislature and no power. All it can do is exhort, plan and hope. A great leader, such as Charles de Gaulle, can shape events and inspire resistance by moral example and force of character. The Greek prime minister in exile was cast in a less heroic mould and buffeted by contradictory currents. Mr Tsouderos was a monarchist (although he later declared himself a Republican) but neither EDES nor ELAS wanted the king back. Both Churchill and Eden did: Britain's long-term strategy for Greece was based on the twin pillars of opposition to communism and restoration of the monarchy, although in the short term Britain was prepared to support any group, of any political colour, that would actively oppose the Germans. Mr Tsouderos was (quite respectfully) told what to do and say by Rex Leeper; he was then replaced and largely forgotten. Novikov, the Soviet Ambassador to Greece, remarked that Leeper, Churchill's agent, was the real prime minister of Greece.[17]

Mr Tsouderos sent the text of his broadcast to the Greek ambassadors in Washington and Moscow to try to gain American and Russian support. The Foreign Office also sent a secret telegram to the British embassies in Washington and Moscow (with a copy to Leeper), which concluded:

> You will notice that Colonel Woodhouse, the senior British Officer in Greece, considers that any delay in exploiting this favourable atmosphere might be fatal. Force of M. Tsouderos' appeal would be immensely strengthened if he could quote approval of the three governments. For our part, we are very ready to give such approval and we very much hope that the Soviet Government and the United States will also agree with the least possible delay to endorse Mr Tsouderos' statement.[18]

On Christmas Day, Ambassador Balfour passed back Moscow's reply:

> Not having the necessary information about the situation in Greece, and not being au courant with all the events which have taken place among the Greek guerrillas, the Soviet Government are unable at the present time to express their opinion on M. Tsouderos' appeal about the uniting of the various partisan groups on occupied Greek territory, which are fighting among themselves.[19]

Leeper commented that:

> Refusal of the Soviet Government to support M. Tsouderos' appeal can hardly be ascribed purely to ignorance of what has been happening in Greece. It is inconceivable that the Soviet Government should be

unaware of close connections between Tito, the LNC [Lëvizja Nacional Çlirimtare, the Communist-controlled National Liberation Front] in Albania, and EAM in Greece, and of the probability that their ultimate aim is to establish a group of Socialist Republics in the Balkans under the aegis of Russia. Mr Molotov [Soviet Minister of Foreign Affairs] may be prepared to watch these developments with a friendly interest without direct interference, but when he is asked to assist the Greek Government in producing a solution in Greece which would obviously be opposed to EAM's solution, his ignorance of Greek affairs can hardly be a full explanation of his refusal.[20]

To his credit, Eden did not give up easily. He summoned the Soviet ambassador in London, Fedor Gusev, who 'asked for an explanation of EDES and EAM and said that his Government spoke the literal truth when they said they had no information at all about the Greek situation.' Eden was silkily diplomatic; he wasn't asking the Soviets to take sides or even comment on the political situation, only to encourage the guerrilla bands 'in their present inclination to unite'. If Molotov did not wish to make a statement, even 'an inspired passage' in the Russian newspaper *Izvestia* would be much better than nothing.[21] The next evening, Balfour met Molotov to hand over a memorandum, restating Britain's argument in favour of reconciliation between EDES and EAM/ELAS. Molotov met every argument with the statement that the Soviet government lacked any information of their own about the situation in Greece. The Russians were not going to be helpful.[22]

Eden's position towards ELAS had changed completely. Rather than abandon them, Britain should be prepared to renew its backing:

> If civil war can be brought to an end I trust that early action will be taken to support the guerrillas. I should favour sending food, clothes and medical supplies to ELAS bands in areas where they are in need, as well as to EDES, to the limit allowed by our resources in aircraft. I consider that arms should also be sent to ELAS in areas where they are resisting the enemy.[23]

Relief sorties to help the refugees from the burned villages continued in the New Year and, as January wore on, preparations began for the resumption of guerrilla action. Hammond had left Pendalofos just after Christmas, making his way south to ELAS HQ, leaving Captain Ronald Prentice in command of Boodle. Pat was itching to get out and reconnoitre targets identified by Eggs: 'the quicker we get to work on them the better. And the sooner we sever connections with the *Andartes* the better too, and become a straightforward sabotage and demolitions organization, with a watching brief on politics. But that will never happen.' Supplies of military equipment resumed; twenty-two containers of explosives, which had been dropped by parachute, came down from the mountain on 20 January and were put in the cellar to be checked. Pat's notes recorded 6,000 sticks of '808' high explosive, weighing a total of 1,500lb, packed 300 to a container.[24]

Pat was busy organizing and running another commando training school. Although ELAS had been quick enough to send 1,000 men from Pendalofos to fight against EDES, it was less keen on training to fight the Germans. There was a good deal of wrangling about attendance, explosives and rounds of ammunition. Pat lectured on fuses, detonators and primers 'to a scruffy, weak, undisciplined class of thirty-three *Andartes*, the worst I have instructed so far; useless as fighting troops'. At the end of the first morning session, he had to break off to deal with a group of Russians held by ELAS. There were only a few Russians in Macedonia: some had joined the Germans voluntarily; others had been captured by them. These were keen to fight the Germans but refused to take part in the civil war; ELAS disowned them, making them a British problem. It fell to Pat, as a trained intelligence officer, to interrogate them with the help of a Russian-speaking Greek, an 'unreliable little man, delicate and self-contained as a bird in all his movements, with a deep husky voice and a melodious Russian accent... He used to be a régisseur [theatre director] in Moscow. What a mix-up this war is.'

Pendalofos was gloomy; the clothes and faces of the civilians seemed colourless in the short, dark January days. Both Left and Right were busy publishing propaganda newspapers, each claiming the same virtues and accusing the other of the same crimes and failures. It would have been amusing, except that it divided the Greeks and allowed the Germans to burn the villages, which was not at all amusing. The visits from village committees were now genuine and distressing; the women from one village camped on the floor and wept and refused to go.[25]

Towards the end of January, the commando training became more ambitious, ending with a practical exercise to demolish a target in enemy-held territory. Closely watched by Pat, the platoon practised laying and then lifting mines, reconnoitred the target and placed charges; their performance was '*very* slow.'

Relations with the ELAS commanders had become more cordial. Greeks and British held a musical evening, during which an Italian tenor sang. The little general got tight and dozed off:

> He woke up at odd moments, usually the wrong moment. At the word
> signorina in one of the songs he gave a start and exclaimed: 'Ah! Signorina!
> Yes, yes! Signorina! Good! Yes!' which made everyone burst out laughing
> and completely put the singer off his stroke... The evening ended with a

furious round dance, the little general beating Zote's behind with a Sam Browne, which he was afterwards too drunk to put on again and had to stuff in his pocket.

Pat was particularly struck by Rennos Michaleas, the *politikos* [political commissar] of ELAS Ninth Division:

> Rennos appeared a nicer, more interesting person than I had realized, though I already liked him. Sitting with his mud-coloured, leonine face between a lamp and a decanter of black wine, with wreathes of smoke blowing across in front of him, he showed himself as a man of quick warm perception, a man of destiny, a man on whom life can play awful tricks and bring extraordinary rewards (not necessarily the material ones) because he has more possibilities. I don't think however he will suffer any catastrophe – long imprisonment, torture, assassination or anything of that sort. He is one of the lucky people who, through no doing of their own, manage to slip aside when catastrophe plunges at them and threatens to run them down. I wonder what all this ELAS business, in which he holds a high place, means to him. Not very much I should think, though he thinks it does. He has much more in him than he knows, but I don't think he will ever realize it or amount to anything much.[26]

Rennos came from a family of wealthy landowners in Mani, on the southern tip of the Peloponnese. His father had studied in Athens and Switzerland before becoming a doctor. Although he held strong liberal-democratic views and was elected as an MP, he did not reject his son when, in his teens, he joined the party and became a committed communist. After Metaxas seized power as dictator of Greece and banned political parties in 1936, the security services pursued suspected communists with vigour and imagination. Rennos was arrested and sent to prison. During the first part of the war, when Russia and the Nazis were allies, the party line was that prisoners should not try to escape; when the Germans bombed a prison transport train, the KKE men gave themselves up to their guards. After the German invasion of Russia in June 1941, the line changed, allowing Rennos to escape and join the Resistance.[27]

At the start of February 1944, Lieutenant Colonel Edmonds arrived at Boodle to take over command both of the station and of the Allied Military Mission activities in Western Macedonia as a whole. Pat was sent to Grevena to construct an airfield. In France, the SOE used the Lysander light aircraft, which hardly needed a runway; operations in Greece, at greater range, needed an airstrip that could take a DC3.

Pat chose a location about 7 kilometres outside Grevena and 3 kilometres from the village of Mavranei, just off the rough road that led south towards Thessaly. It was a good spot. Grevena had been 'liberated' from the Italians in July 1943; although the Germans had burned the town in December, they had withdrawn again, and the road was so bad that wheeled transport could get no closer than a four-hour march, so there was no risk of a surprise attack. However, any German operations in the area would hold up the work, since many of the workers belonged to the ELAS Reserve and would be called for duty if there were an attack. Villagers still remember the airstrip and the British; Captain Evans, it is said, lived in a hut near the site, under a stand of trees close to a spring of running water.

Pat recruited a competent Greek civilian builder, who prepared a detailed scale plan for an airfield just over 1 kilometre long by 200 metres wide, with a central 600-metre landing and take-off zone. Pat calculated how long it would take to clear the scrub, grub out roots and fill holes; to level and fill the road and tracks where they ran across the runway; to level hummocks and fill hollows and ditches with gravel, sand and earth reinforced with twigs; and to lay field drains. Women could cut twigs and dig, but not grub out roots or cut down trees. Horse-drawn carts and mules with panniers would be needed to bring gravel and earth. A man's labour cost more than a woman's (one-tenth of a sovereign per day as opposed to one-twelfth), but less than a mule (one-eighth of a sovereign per day) or a horse and cart (one-fifth of a sovereign per day). The whole job should take about 2,000 days' work (including men, women and mule 'days'), costing up to 250 sovereigns. There was no shortage of local labour, but the availability of mission supervisors would be a limiting factor: 'these are Greek workers and always want to do things their own way even when it is patently wrong and against all instructions. Therefore they need constant supervision.' An officer and the competent Greek foreman could between them manage a workforce of 300. With two extra supervisors, that could be increased to 700. The supervisors would not have to be officers or speak Greek. British NCOs, or even escaped prisoners of war awaiting evacuation from the mission, could do the job if they were well-briefed, had thick skins and were prepared to walk incessantly up and down watching, cursing and demonstrating.

The worst problem was the weather. Rain had followed the snow and by early February, the site was waterlogged and unworkable. Very little could be done until fine weather came to dry the ground, but rain and snow continued to fall. After about a fortnight, Pat was joined by an American flyer, Lieutenant Hughling, who had returned from southern Yugoslavia in the company of ELAS's leading political figure, Andreas Tzimas, who went by the *nom de guerre* of Samariniotis. Hughling was trying to get out of the Balkans and return to his unit. This was easier said than done and he stayed on in Grevena to take over the airfield construction after Pat left. Samariniotis had been trying to contact the Yugoslav partisan leadership to discuss the future of Macedonia. Colonel Woodhouse (the senior SOE officer in Greece) believed that Samariniotis was also trying to drive a wedge between the British and Americans by persuading Hughling that the British were frustrating his efforts to return to Italy and that the Yugoslav partisans would be able to help. The plan backfired and Hughling's experiences on the trip brought the Americans to share the British distrust of ELAS.[28]

Samariniotis came from Kastoria; he was well-educated and spoke Greek, Vlach, Bulgarian, Serbo-Croat and several other languages. Before the war, he had been in and out of prison for his communist beliefs and received political education in Moscow. He became Athens Party Secretary and in 1941 was one of the founding leaders of EAM and ELAS. Samariniotis was the most intellectual of the Greek communist leaders. Pat found him

> exquisitely neat, a suave talker, pleasant-mannered, and with curiously involuted mind, always developing fresh possibilities and combinations, a mind to which both intrigue, with its betrayals and negotiations, with their pokerfaced duplicity, were probably second nature. Of the various ELAS personalities I have met, high and low, he is one of the few who stands out as at all interesting in himself. But he was not a man of really large character.[29]

During the bad weather of February, Pat found the time to write to Jill, who was having a difficult time. Her health was poor, with constant colds and flu. Her brother Jim had ruptured a lung in a diving experiment, her best friend was having a marital crisis, and Jill was unhappy because at the age of 30 her hair was beginning to go grey. Pat wrote a sequence of a dozen letters, which passed through the censor in Cairo in a batch on 22 May before being sent on to Jill in London. How did they leave Greece? Were they collected from the airstrip he was building? Or were they taken out by an officer slipping away from the coast, by submarine? However they got there, the letters were full of love, reassurance and admonitions to take care of herself, complemented by visions of a peaceful rural married life together after the war.

While based at Grevena, Pat bought mules and fodder to support the campaign to harass the Germans and worked with ELAS on plans for ambushes and demolition in the pass to the east, through which German forces would withdraw. He also visited Dotsiko to report on the condition of the Italian prisoners of war, who were still camping out; ELAS would not allow them to live in villages and they could buy nothing locally except salt, oil, lentils, beans, chick-peas, raisins and sugar. ELAS had ordered them not to buy wheat or maize in Grevena but to send civilians (selected by ELAS) to buy supplies further away in German-occupied areas. ELAS fixed the prices, and changed the sovereigns provided by the British for their support. There was dysentery in the camp and more than eighty cases of malaria; men would die if they were not given medicine.[30]

Chapter Three

Fertiliser: The Station on Vitsi

The March from Pendalofos to Vapsori.

By March 1944, the British had cautiously renewed military and financial support to ELAS in preparation for operations against a German withdrawal. Pat left the landing strip at Grevena for other hands to complete when the weather improved. On his return to Boodle, he was promoted to captain and ordered to go north to establish a new station, code-named 'Fertiliser', on the heights of Mount Vitsi.

Vitsi rose to more than 2,100 metres, overlooking the strategic routes to Albania and Yugoslavia, in the heart of German-occupied territory. To the north-east, the town of Florina was not only a major garrison but also a railhead and the crossroads for communications between the German Army Group E in Yugoslavia and Army Group F in Salonika. The railway, and the road through from Florina to Albania, protected by guard posts and block houses in the passes, allowed the Germans to move large bodies of fighting men, matériel and support troops rapidly across Western Macedonia. To the south-west, the Wehrmacht maintained lesser garrisons at Kastoria and at Argos Orestikon, which commanded the Aliakmon valley.

Pat would need the support of the local population to survive in territory where betrayal to the occupiers or their collaborators would be fatal. However, the local population was fantastically mixed with an extraordinary number of linguistic, cultural and religious populations jumbled together. Western Macedonia had been part of the Ottoman Empire and had only formally become Greek thirty years before, after the end of the Balkan War in 1913. Under the Ottomans, peasants were fixed to their land, village schoolmasters and administrators were tied to their official posts, but the landless population ebbed and flowed through the mountains between what would become Greece, Albania, Yugoslavia and Bulgaria. States and borders had been fuzzy concepts in an Empire where people moved for trade, for grazing, for work as craftsmen or labourers, as itinerant musicians or bandits. Since then, communities and identities had been horribly fractured by the forced population exchanges of hundreds of thousands after the 'Great Disaster' of Greece's defeat by Turkey in 1923.

To make matters worse, Kastoria was the main centre of the 'Axis-Macedonian Bulgarian Committee' and its armed militia, the *Komitadji*, set up by the Bulgarians and Italians in March 1943.[1] For the Italians and Germans, the *Komitadji* were a means of reducing the number of their own troops needed to hold down the occupied territory. For Bulgaria, which had already absorbed large swathes of Greek Eastern Macedonia, the *Komitadji* were a means towards further territorial expansion in northern Greece.

In this northern corner of the country, jammed up against the Albanian and Yugoslav borders, the majority of the inhabitants spoke a Slavic language as their mother tongue, with Greek as a second, third or even fourth language. Ethnic Greeks soon labelled any Slav-speaker who opposed the Resistance a *Komitadji* whether he had anything to do with the Bulgarians or not,[2] but the reality was far more complex and fluid. Some of the so-called *Komitadjis* were not pro-Axis or pro-Bulgar but simply wanted an independent Macedonia. Some did not quite know what they wanted but did not like the Greeks. Others had been forced by the Germans, or persuaded by German and Bulgarian propaganda, to take up arms against ELAS. Finally, there were a few who were fanatically pro-Bulgar and wanted a Bulgarian Macedonia. By 1944, *Komitadji* militias were established in many of the villages between Kastoria and Florina. There they guarded roads and bridges, provided the Germans with intelligence, helped their patrols search for arms and joined them in actions against ELAS. The *Komitadjis* were well-armed and fought stubbornly, particularly in defence of their villages, although they seldom attacked the *Andartes* on their own.

Peter Kite had been promoted to sergeant. Pat described him as 'tall and bony and well built, with terrific energy and a red face, a long jaw and a sense of humour. The achievement of being a first-rate NCO is something which he takes as it were in his stride. There is a lot to him.'[3] Although he spoke no Greek, Kite was one of those rare, imperturbable men who seemed able to get on with anyone and make his way anywhere. Sent out on reconnaissance in February, he had identified the village of Vapsori as the best site for a northern base, at an altitude of 1,250 metres on the flank of Vitsi, away from roads but surrounded by a web of tracks and paths. Vapsori was also the headquarters of the 'Vitsi Detachment of 9th Division ELAS', raised during the previous winter from the surrounding Slav-speaking villages by a commander known as Arrianos, the *nom de guerre* of Aristoteles Choutouras who came from the Voion village of Leukothea. Pat's orders were to contact the Vitsi detachment, discover its strength and condition, its needs for arms and clothing, and its operational effectiveness. He was to gather intelligence about the enemy in Florina and Amyndeo to the west, and identify targets to attack in Operation NOAH'S ARK in order to 'disrupt enemy forces withdrawing from Greece so that they cannot reach another theatre of war without large scale reorganization.' In the meantime, he should carry out preparatory commando and sabotage operations.

Vapsori is only about 50 kilometres from Pendalofos as the crow flies. On the ground, it was a march of 120 kilometres. Pat set off with a little party of three soldiers, ten muleteers and eleven mules at midday on 21 March. The weather was foul and the tracks filthy; the party got no further that night than the village of Polikastano, about 20 kilometres away. Where the track ran along a high ridge, the mules repeatedly sank up to their bellies in the deep snow, got stuck, broke their girths and had to be extricated, reloaded and coaxed forward again.

In the morning, the group divided. Pat's Greek wireless operator, Corporal Manitsoudhis, took the mules, radio set and supplies on a lower, longer path to avoid the worst of the snow. Pat himself set off on foot, with one companion, on a direct route over the high mountains to the village of Nestorio. On the way, he met ELAS's 1st Battalion, 28th Regiment, who had been fighting the right-wing nationalist EDES resistance forces in Epiros. The *Andartes* were singing to keep their spirits up, but they looked very tired, cold and ragged. Most of them were going back to quarters, although their commander, Lytridhis, would bring a contingent to join Pat on Mount Vitsi. Pat pushed on and spent the night in almost the only house in the village of Upper Nestorio that had not been burned by the Germans the previous October.

Corporal Manitsoudhis's column reached the village in the middle of the next morning, after an eventful journey. The civilian muleteers had gone on strike in a remote spot and threatened to dump their loads in the snow and leave unless they got more pay. Manitsoudhis had drawn his pistol and threatened to shoot them. Pat was furious. The muleteers had been engaged at the standard rate of one-eighth of a sovereign per mule per day loaded on the way out, one-sixteenth of a sovereign unloaded on the return. They were also getting their food, cigarettes and fodder for the mules, which was generous. Pat gave them a monumental dressing-down. After that, there were no more complaints or demands, however bad the cold, the snow or the mud.

Nestorio was the last outpost of 'Free Greece', the ELAS stronghold that the Germans rarely bothered to enter. Beyond the Aliakmon to the north was enemy-controlled territory where Pat and his column would have to take care to conceal their presence. The Germans were in both Kastoria and the little town of Argos Orestikon, there were guard posts on the roads, and the way to Vapsori lay across a plain sprinkled with *Komitadji* villages.

Nestorio was also a language frontier, marking the start of the Slavophone region where almost all the villages were Slav with just a few enclaves of Greek or Turkish-speaking refugees from Asia Minor. Most Greeks suspected the Slav-speakers of supporting the cause of Macedonian independence and referred to them contemptuously as 'Bulgars'. Certainly, the Bulgarians, Italians and Germans had encouraged the Slav-speakers to support the Axis by holding out promises of an independent Macedonia. Tito and his partisans also offered a rival vision of a Macedonia with free speech, free elections, its own language, hospitals and schools, in a federation with Yugoslavia. This, too, was anathema to patriotic Greek communists. To add pepper to the broth, the Albanian 'Ballisti' nationalist bands collaborated with the Germans and stirred up trouble on the Greek side of the border. Pat would be stepping into a seething cauldron of violently competing interests, where it would be almost impossible to tell friend from foe among the native population, where he would be constantly observed and at risk of betrayal to very powerful occupying forces. It was an invigorating prospect.

In Nestorio, Pat asked the local ELAS battalion commander for help. Stavriatos was a man of about 40, who had been a regular officer in the Greek

Air Force and fought in the Albanian campaign. He was not a communist but had 'come to the mountains', as the popular saying went, to fight the Germans. Stavriatos assigned Pat four Slav-speaking *Andartes* as runners and guides. Together they planned a route that would make a wide detour through the foothills skirting the Albanian border on the northern rim of the plain until they reached a comparatively safe point to cross the road and the River Aliakmon and head up towards Mount Vitsi and the village of Vapsori.

After leaving Nestorio, the party slept at Khionato, a Greek refugee village just 7 kilometres away, which was desperately hospitable; it was hard to persuade their host to take money. The next night the party stopped at Dendrochori, a Slav village, which had no hesitation about accepting payment. At nine o'clock the next morning, just as the column was getting ready to leave, an *Andarte* platoon arrived from Vapsori to conduct them over the valley road. However, the *Andartes* had been marching all night and needed to rest before making the return. Pat wanted to get on and left without them. The weather was so bad that no *Komitadji* were likely to be abroad, and the locals said there had been no German movement for several days. It was a rare opportunity to cross the road, the river and the small plain beyond it in daylight and comparative safety. The column passed the mud-brick villages of Kranionas and Mavrokambos, huddled in the open at the edge of the plain, and began to climb again, past the stone houses of Agios Andonios through a sheltered defile between hills. Now they were on a track that wound upwards through a little valley, with a rushing stream to the right and a steep wooded slope to the left. The sharp, damp air was filled with the sound of birdsong. Far ahead, the church of Vapsori stood out against the trees and the pinnacle of Vitsi rose through the cloud and mist, improbably high above. A tiny bridge took the mule path across the stream, where a few inches of clear water bubbled and foamed across a rocky bed between grassy verges sprinkled with daisies and dandelions, before the real climb started. This bit of the path was roughly paved, and a groove had been cut in a shallow spur of rock so that a wheeled cart could pass. Then the path became steeper, twisting between stone houses clinging to the mountainside. To the left of the path, another steep valley opened to show a mountain flank striped with jagged ribs of bare rock.

After four days' hard travelling, the party arrived in the heart of the village on a patch of open ground in front of the school and the church, where they were met by Arrianos. Pat asked for the use of a house, to set up the wireless for the afternoon 'sked' that was due to take place in an hour. For security reasons, SOE radio operators never communicated with other operators or stations in the field but had schedules of prearranged times for transmissions to and from headquarters. Wireless communications between Fertiliser and Boodle had to be relayed through SOE Headquarters in Cairo or southern Italy. To reduce the risk of detection, times were changed and frequencies switched at short intervals. Messages were encrypted using one-time pads to generate unbreakable cipher-text and transmitted as Morse code. All the coding and decoding, and the logjam of signals traffic, caused delays: it was actually quicker to send messages – particularly long and complicated ones – between Fertiliser and Boodle over the mountains by runner.

While Manitsoudhis went off to set up the radio, Arrianos drew Pat aside and said with a smile: 'Look here, you oughtn't to have talked about the wireless like that in front of all the villagers.' Pat said the villagers would know about it soon enough anyway; they would see the aerial and hear the generator. Arrianos looked crestfallen, but agreed.

Security on Vitsi alternated between elaborate precautions that did not matter and neglect of those that did. Leaks were inevitable in an area where it was often impossible to tell friend from enemy and the air was thick with suspicion and conspiracy. It was 'rather fun, provided you did not worry too much' and, in practice, secrecy was less important than good intelligence. The day after arriving, Pat met two men who lived in Florina and would supply regular information about the enemy. He paid 'agents 22 and 23' 2 sovereigns 'in circumstances which did not allow of my taking a receipt.' In future, the spies signed for gold with the pseudonym 'Robert Smith' or 'R. Smith'.[4]

The village was snowed up and more snow was falling steadily, but there was plenty to do before the start of operations. The Vitsi detachment numbered about 550 *Andartes*. Most of them were based at Vapsori, with a contingent at Dendrochori to keep open the supply line to Free Greece. Lytridhis was nominally in command: he dealt with Ninth Division Headquarters and handled the administration. Arrianos, though, was the dominant personality and operational commander, 'an instinctive leader, with just the right amount of fire to make men follow and obey'. Arrianos was eager to win the confidence of the British and to show the keenness and devotion of his *Andartes*, most of whom were in civilian clothes and poorly fed. Pat made page after page of notes about their needs, with estimates of quantities and costs of arms, clothing and maintenance, and questions about the possibility of buying reserves of food and forage. After some haggling, he agreed to pay a maintenance subsidy of 630 sovereigns a month for 550 Andartes, payable in three instalments. Boots would be extra. Footgear was a serious problem. Most of Arrianos's men only had goatskin slippers. The local boot leather was very poor and wore out quickly; nails for the soles were almost unobtainable. Could any British boot soles be supplied? Pat paid Arrianos 50 sovereigns to buy boots for the Vitsi detachment and wrote to Boodle about future supplies. House rent for the station was agreed at a sovereign a month; a Greek private, not an ELAS *Andarte* but a commando from Pendalofos, was entrusted with 20 sovereigns to buy household stores and mule fodder, and 5 more for 'expenses in connection with dispersal of explosives and care of the house'. To Pat's annoyance, the ELAS political junta attended all his meetings and insisted that everything to do with houses, runners, mules, fodder and supplies should be done through them rather than the villagers.

Lieutenant Zotos and Sergeant Kite arrived a week later, together with a medical orderly, Corporal Long, twenty-two Greek commandos who Pat had trained in Pendalofos and a convoy of forty-five mules laden with explosives, some boots and clothes for the *Andartes*. The commando group had been troublesome on the journey. Pat sacked two of their NCOs, gave the rest a lecture and reorganized them into two sections. To undo the effects of 'months of ELAS lack of discipline', he got Pendalofos's agreement to use them in interim operations; although casualties might reduce their numbers before NOAH'S ARK, the remainder would be more effective and reliable.

Action began sooner than planned. A *Komitadji* observation post on the heights between Sidirochori and Agios Andonios had spotted the columns coming up the defile. On 2 April, a company of *Andartes* guarding the eastern approach to Vapsori fought off a small-scale but determined attack by SS troops. ELAS took five prisoners but shot them dead on the way back to Vapsori before Pat could interrogate them.

Two days later, a larger body of SS troops made a concerted drive. The mission party, together with Arrianos, left Vapsori in a hurry at about ten in the morning. There was no time to hide the explosives and other stores properly; with the help of the villagers, they were simply dumped in a small ravine outside Vapsori.

Pat and his men headed up the mountain to heights near the hamlet of Korifi. In the late afternoon they left Korifi and went down to Makrochori, and then up the valley to the little village of Melas which they reached early on the morning of 5 April. Melas is a monument to Greek national pride, renamed in honour of an officer who was killed there in 1904, leading a small band fighting for a Greek Macedonia. There was no time to visit his tomb – a small, bare cell by a stream outside the village – as the enemy was reported to be approaching. So they left again and spent most of the day on the high, snow-covered mountains above the village. During the night, they came down the valley and across the little plain to reach Dendrochori at breakfast time on 6 April after nearly forty-eight hours on the move.

Meanwhile, the *Andartes* stationed on the two main approaches to Vapsori, from the east and west, held off the Germans throughout the first day. By the evening though, the *Andartes* were running out of ammunition and had to withdraw. A third group of about seventy Germans and *Komitadjis* approached Vapsori up a track from the south, past the armed village of Sidirochori. Arrianos did not have enough men to cover a simultaneous assault from three directions and in the afternoon of 4 April, five of the attackers entered Vapsori unopposed.

The village was almost deserted. The only males left were an old man and a travelling musician who had worked in Italy, Bulgaria, Yugoslavia and Greece before the war. The Germans shot the old man and arrested the musician. They took a few pack animals and a little food, which they ate as they searched the village before withdrawing late in the afternoon. The next day, a column of about seventy men from the SS group entered Vapsori from the west. After searching the village again, they pretended to leave but camped among trees nearby. In the morning, the attackers finally withdrew; the villagers had told them nothing and they had failed to discover Fertiliser's explosives and stores.

The Vitsi detachment regrouped at Dendrochori but Arrianos would not go back to Vapsori until he had more ammunition. Pat waited with him, using the opportunity to gather intelligence about political and military tensions. ELAS immediately provided a lesson by recalling one of the *Andartes* attached to Pat's group. Pat wanted to hold on to the man, who was cheerful, bold and a useful linguist. ELAS, though, wanted him for political work in *Komitadji* villages, spreading propaganda, beating up dissenters and killing traitors. According to ELAS, he had even been the organizing secretary of the *Komitadji* in his village and it was necessary to test his reliability. It sounded contradictory but there were many cases of men changing sides. ELAS may also have been worried that he would absorb royalist ideas from the British. In replacement, Arrianos provided a young *Andarte* and an older man. Judas Aaron was a middle-aged ginger-haired Greek Jew who had served in a British canteen in Salonika in the Great War and spoke a little broken English. He was soon nicknamed 'Joe' and proved to be 'a staunch old rogue' who could be entrusted with critical tasks.

After a few days, Pat wrote back to Colonel Edmonds that the area around Vitsi was solidly anti-royalist.[5] It would not be a welcoming place for any of the Greek officers attached to the mission: EAM and many of the inhabitants would see them as royalist spies. Pat's own line with EAM officials and ELAS officers was to avoid political discussion by saying: 'I am a simple soldier and politics neither concern nor interest me. My work is purely military. So are my orders. What interests me is beating the enemy.' The 'Organization' (as the British sometimes referred to the EAM/ELAS/Communist Party nexus) didn't believe this for a minute. There was a widespread belief that the British planned to restore the king and Pat had already been wrongly suspected of sympathy with Zervas (the leader of the right-wing resistance EDES) whom ELAS accused of collusion with the Germans. Now, ELAS suspected Pat of favouring Macedonian autonomy.[6] Pat's interests, both as a trained Intelligence officer and an intellectual with a well-developed sense of political history, may not have been those of a 'simple soldier' but his job was purely military. He had no political remit and no hidden agenda. As he wrote in a secret report to the Foreign Office: 'Our problem, I take it, is to get our targets in NOAH'S ARK; that and nothing more. We are not, fortunately, entrusted with the task of solving the political problems of the Balkans.'[7] Although he felt that the Slav *Andartes* tended to fight with more guts than their Greek comrades, he avoided making any distinction between Greek and Slav and tried to show that the British were friendly towards anyone who helped the Allies.

Liaison officers had to navigate the turbulent currents of Balkan politics, tensions between different language groups, left and right, communist, fascist, nationalist and royalist interests, and local perceptions of Great Power policies. The region had only become part of the Greek state in 1913 after the Second Balkan War. Most of the people were Slavs and spoke a Slav dialect as their mother tongue, with Greek as a second or third language. The political situation among the Slav-speaking population was complex, fluid and bedevilled by suspicions, including an illusion that Britain might unite with Germany to turn against Russia. Pat wrote that

England is regarded rather as a plutocracy than a democracy. While I do not personally like the ultimate aims of the inner leaders of EAM, I must admit that EAM has done and is doing a very useful thing for us, from a military point of view, in converting wavering Slav villages from Bulgarian to Greek allegiance.[8]

Pat categorized the Slav-speaking villages into three groups as follows:

- '*Komitadji* villages' were armed by the Bulgarians or Germans; their militia would certainly report the mission's position to the Germans and might attack them and the *Andartes*.
- 'Converted villages' had been won over by propaganda, or cowed into submission after being invaded and disarmed by ELAS, with executions of 'traitors'. A kind of 'pseudo-communism' was strong among them, the *Internationale* was sung and the clenched hand was sometimes raised in greeting. However, there was little real knowledge of communism, which was vaguely associated with the idealized vision of a 'People's Democracy' promoted by EAM and the Communist Party. The conversion was often fragile and allegiances could change again. Polykeraso, which had been converted and was friendly in February, had since been re-armed by the Germans.
- 'Loyal villages' had fully accepted EAM-ELAS and supported the idea of a war of liberation.

Most villagers were anti-royalist, because they associated the king with the repressive measures of Metaxas; they liked the Left's hatred of the king. Although most of EAM and ELAS in the area were Red, there was no reason to suppose that

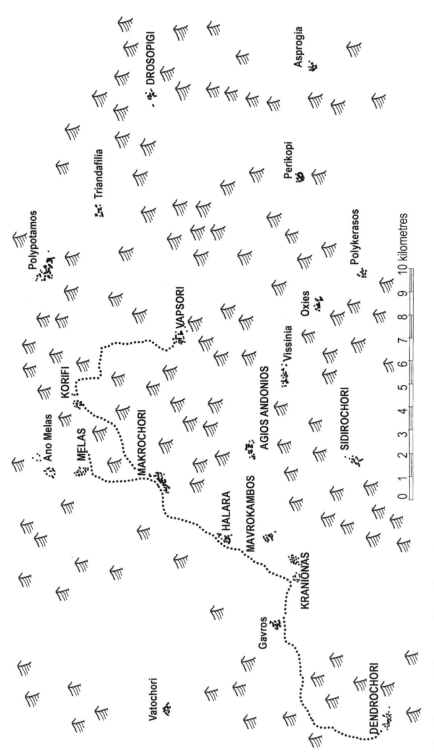

Fertiliser and the attack on Vapsori.

people here would like Communism if they got it. They do not know what it is and only think they would like it. The average Greek here as in most other parts of the country is a peasant and thinks of three acres and a cow – his own cow. He would hate to be collectivized.

In practice, the allegiance of a Slav Macedonian village at any moment was closely related to who held the local power and which power group (German, *Komitadji* or EAM/ELAS) exercised the greatest threat. EAM/ELAS tried to counter both the *Komitadji* and Slav Partisan influence by promoting an organization called the 'Slav-Macedonian National Liberation Front' or SNOF for short. However, Pat thought that SNOF was not so much a Macedonian nationalist organization as EAM (a Greek organization) using the Slav language, re-badged with a Slav name. It was all very complicated, made more so by changes of allegiance that reflected shifts in power, local resentments and the pursuit of blood feuds.

The attack on Vapsori had shown that it was only safe to send stores from Pendalofos by night. Supply dumps must be kept secret and Fertiliser had to be ready to move at very short notice. Buying mules or fodder in the area was dangerous: sovereigns brought people like flies round a honey-pot and spread rumours of the mission's presence. Pat asked for as much ammunition as possible: there would be some fighting around Vitsi before NOAH'S ARK and a great deal during NOAH'S ARK itself. Vitsi threatened the communications artery northward to Yugoslavia through the Monastir Gap, so the Germans would probably either make a drive or two into the area to paralyse the *Andartes* as a fighting force, or occupy the villages on the fringe of the area as a preliminary to evacuation. The station would need a runner to carry letters and reports that were too long to transmit by wireless and too important or sensitive to entrust to an ELAS runner. Sergeant Kite needed a Slav-Greek-English interpreter and everybody would like tinned food, tinned milk, dried milk, tea, coffee, sugar, English cigarettes, chocolate, concentrated foods, marmalade and jam. 'These are a godsend when on the run.'

Pat also wrote a less formal letter to Captain Ronald Prentice, bubbling over with enthusiasm for his new command, his mission and life in the mountains. After setting out plans for an attack on the towns of Florina and Kastoria to plot German positions, he signed off with an invitation to 'come up here soonest, you'll love it.'

Pat, Arrianos, the companies of *Andartes* and the mule train of ammunition travelled back to Vitsi overnight, arriving on 14 April. Pat stored the explosives and a reserve of food in a well outside the village and gave the ammunition to Arrianos. Welcome though it was, the ammunition was only enough to fight off two German attacks, at most: it was not enough to allow the *Andartes* to make any attacks themselves. Pendalofos was a long way from Vitsi, ammunition was heavy and a mule could only carry a load of 150 to 200lb; Arrianos was held in check for fear of exhausting his ammunition.

The villagers were now scared but friendly. The musician had been released and returned to Vapsori after just a few days in captivity. However, three or four weeks later, ELAS marched him off to Free Greece, where he was almost certainly put to death as a spy. Although the Slav *Andartes* liked his songs about the freedom of Macedonia, he had already been suspect to ELAS as a Bulgar. His release by the Germans added to the suspicion and the *Andartes* said he had admitted telling the Germans there was a party of British in Vapsori with a wireless set.

Vapsori suddenly became very full of people: on 17 April, two Macedonian brigades of Tito's Yugoslav partisans arrived, accompanied by a British liaison officer, Captain MacDonald. The first brigade was moving from Mount Kaimaktsalan, on the Greek-Yugoslav border east of Florina, to an area in Yugoslavia close to Lake Ohrid and the border with Albania. The second brigade was there as an escort, to make diversionary attacks, seize and hold difficult passes so the first brigade could get through unmolested. The two brigades had succeeded in crossing the Florina plain by night, slipping past the German forces unnoticed. They had come to Vapsori on their way to the Prespa Lakes, which span the border between Greece and Albania. From Prespa, they would head north again through the mountains towards the town of Ohrid, on the banks of Lake Ohrid in Yugoslav Macedonia. The partisans had a particularly good system of runners: each of the main supply and communications routes had a dedicated patrol, which 'knew the route to perfection, was always up-to-date regarding enemy posts, knew all the villages and villagers on and near the route, all the springs and wells and so on.'

Pat was impressed and invigorated: here was a serious fighting force and that would be a real menace to the Germans. Although many of them were badly clothed and shod, they held themselves like soldiers. They did not scrounge weapons and they fought bravely. There were a few girls with the partisans – some as nurses, some as fighting troops – who went everywhere with the men, marching through the thick snow with no boots, only stockings. Morals were very strict and the humour was clean.

Captain MacDonald introduced Pat to Deyan, the leader of the Yugoslav partisans in the Prespa area, and to Abbas, political commissar of all Tito's Macedonian units. Deyan was recruiting round the Prespa Lakes and sending men back to Ohrid, where they were equipped, trained and enrolled in existing partisan units. He was having to turn away applicants for lack of arms and clothes, but would be able to form a Prespa brigade if the British could provide explosives, gold and clothes. Pat liked the idea. During NOAH'S ARK, the *Andartes* would have heavy commitments in the Klidhi Pass on the main rail and road routes to the east of Florina. The mission was afraid there would not be enough men to also deal with the vital stretch of road running west from Florina to Albania. However, this was not a straightforward military question. There were tensions between ELAS and the partisans, between Greeks and Slavs, and Tito's post-war intentions were unclear; the future control of Macedonia was at stake.

During their visit, the Yugoslav partisan leaders addressed a gathering in Vapsori and invited the Greek Slav Macedonians to enlist with them, rather than with ELAS, to further the cause of the 'Slav Macedonian People'.[9] Arrianos, in return, invited the partisans to join him in an attack on the armed village of Perikopi, just over the mountain to the south-west. Abbas, the partisan commander, refused. When Cairo turned down the scheme to create a partisan brigade in Prespa, Pat reluctantly recognized the wisdom of the decision. Rivalry between Greek and Slav Macedonians was a dangerous distraction.

Arrianos's men now embarked on a series of small-scale actions. A band of Armenians had come across from the garrison at Vatochori (roughly halfway between Mount Vitsi and the Albanian border) to steal food at Kranionas on the little plain at the foot of the mountain. *Andarte* detachments surrounded the village, killed two Armenians and captured seven more. Pat interrogated the captives briefly before they were taken away to Pendalofos.

Arrianos then decided to attack Perikopi without the partisans. Pat wanted to see how he performed in action, but was entirely taken up with the Yugoslav partisans, planning sessions with Captain MacDonald and the seemingly endless administration associated with running a station. Sergeant Kite went in his place.

Arrianos and Lytridhis planned the operation together; Lytridhis wrote the orders and Arrianos led the assault. Kite reported that the *Andartes* showed excellent discipline under fire. Arrianos thought quickly and was not afraid to switch his forces when he saw things going wrong; the company and platoon commanders reflected his boldness and vigour. The defenders had been no pushover and opened fire almost immediately the attack started, showing that they had been sleeping in their clothes with their weapons at their bedside. The *Komitadji* speedily launched a counter-attack from the neighbouring village of Sidirochori, forcing the *Andartes* to withdraw after burning fifteen houses. Ten days later, on the night of 28/29 April, Pat and one section of his commandos accompanied Arrianos's battalion on an attack on Sidirochori; night attacks were far more difficult and this assault was not so successful.

It was clear that Arrianos's battalion was a good one, the *Komitadji* was a military element to be reckoned with, and the local villagers were in a horrible position. Whichever side they supported, they were liable to get their houses burned and paid a heavy toll in food and livestock. They would be in danger from every shift of power among their enemies, as well as from quislings and turncoats.

In May, a small German attack on a nearby village, Polypotamos, was preceded by the approach of three civilians. They were stopped by the sentries, who were women as there were no *Andartes* in the village. The sentries would not let them through without passes. The three men asked to be taken to the local head of the 'Organization' so they could establish their bona fides and get passes to continue their journey. Eventually the women agreed. When the men were brought to the responsible person, they produced revolvers, held him up and escorted him to the Germans, who came out from their hiding place and entered the village.

Pat cultivated his Florina agents and sent Cairo a flow of signals with detailed accounts of enemy strengths, troop movements by road and rail, goods traffic and targets for air attack. At the end of April, Edmonds instructed him to concentrate on 'auxiliary targets such as petrol dumps' and passed on a directive from Cairo to 'prevent withdrawal of further Hun troops from Greece' by 'attacks on opportunity targets such as small road convoys or detachments, railway engines, derailments etc.' They should: 'Capture enemy equipment for use by guerrillas. Reduce risks of reprisals to minimum, and try to kill those responsible for their organization.' This was easier said than done: Pat only had twenty commandos of his own and the *Andartes* were distracted by disputes with the Yugoslav partisans.

While the *Andartes* were attacking Sidirochori, partisans had attacked the German-Armenian garrison protecting the Vigla Pisoderi pass on the road from Florina to the Prespa Lakes; after the attack, the Germans reinforced the garrison. Lytridhis and Arrianos were furious; EAM/ELAS had been trying to persuade the Armenians to desert en masse, with all their arms, ammunition and mules. The partisans had not consulted them and had no right to conduct operations on Greek soil without ELAS permission. The partisans were also, they said, commandeering more food than the villagers could afford and making anti-Greek propaganda to the Slav-speaking population.

Pat found this story plausible and worrying. Lack of co-ordination, let alone serious trouble between ELAS and partisans, could spoil the plans for NOAH'S ARK. Pisoderi was an ARK target and conflict there would attract German drives that the Vitsi battalion could not hope to repel. Pat sent a note to the partisan commander in Trivouno, asking him to make no more attacks in ELAS areas without consultation.

Arrianos and Lytridhis had been plotting and on the night of 5 May launched an operation against enemy posts held by Armenians, with a stiffening of German officers, all the way from the Vigla Pass to Viglista, just over the Albanian border. Their plan was to persuade the Armenians to desert, kill or capture the Germans and take their arms, ammunition, pack animals and supplies. Political organizations in the villages had prepared the ground by delicate undercover work. Eventually about 200 men came over, in twos and threes, to the *Andartes* during the following week and a fair quantity of arms, ammunition and equipment was taken.

The attack on the Armenian garrisons was bound to invite reprisals. The Germans had already caught six buyers working for the Vitsi detachment in Florina and made a swoop on surrounding villages, checking identity cards and making arrests. Arrianos could not possibly hold out for long against a serious enemy drive. Concealment, not defence, would be the only protection.

Fertiliser had grown further with the addition of Major Norman Astell of the Raiding Support Regiment (RSR). Cairo had created the RSR to provide heavy weapons support for the Resistance in Yugoslavia and Greece. Astell had parachuted into Western Macedonia as part of a small advance party to contact the mission, survey targets and make plans for NOAH'S ARK. He had been making for Fertiliser when he was ambushed by *Komitadjis* just after dawn on 3 May; his group had scattered in all directions. Pat met Astell by chance at Drosopigi, a village 13 kilometres west of Vapsori, and took him back over the mountain paths to Fertiliser to discuss targets and tactics. Pat's party was now thirty-seven strong, too many to move and hide in the presence of the enemy. So, on the evening of 8 May, he split the group. Fertiliser's headquarters, with Kite, the radio and its operator Sergeant Leo Voller, ten commandos, one *Andarte* and seven mules went into the woods with enough food for three weeks. The rest of the party went west, across the River Aliakmon and the road, to Dendrochori, to wait for the arrival of the RSR and ammunition for the *Andartes*; the Italian mule drivers, who had been having a miserable time, went back to Pendalofos. They had worked hard but could not get on with the Greek pack saddles, the *Andartes* did not like them, Pat could not arm them, and unarmed they felt insecure. Dependable muleteers were essential to the mission: the Greek muleteers recruited in Pendalofos were now committed members of the team and it was a matter of great pride to be trusted with the radio on one side of the mule, balanced with gold sovereigns on the other. 'Whatever happens,' Pat used to say, 'don't lose the radio. As long as we have the radio we can always get more gold. Without the radio, we are stuck.'[10]

There was less snow on the mountains now: it was possible, though not pleasant, to live outdoors. Vitsi's woods were mostly beech, with a little oak but no pine. Beech woods are cold and wet but they have thick foliage, which would give good cover until the end of October. Fertiliser would be safer in the woods than in the village, harder to find and better placed to evade an enemy drive. From his camp, Pat wrote a long letter to Edmonds about his plans and needs. He did not have enough explosives to attack the designated targets, but even gunpowder would be useful for blowing up roads; he hoped to start photographing targets, using the camera his Florina agents had bought, but the film would have to be developed in Pendalofos; and he wanted to set up a regular runner service between Fertiliser and Boodle.

Late in the afternoon of 11 May, the camp's observation post spotted a *Komitadji* column, armed with rifles, about a quarter of a mile away. The group hid all the essential stores deep in the woods and took up positions. Pat then went up to the observation post to investigate but the column was no longer in sight. The enemy had approached and skirted Vapsori before climbing the heights near Sidirochori, fired a few shots in the general direction of the *Andarte* post at Agios Andonios and made off. The *Komitadjis* probably just wanted to discover *Andarte* positions and make a display to impress the villagers. The display of strength was an effective psychological device and an essential part of warfare in the mountains, where unarmed civilians were quite as much a factor as the various military forces. Even in *Andarte* strongholds such as Vapsori, the villagers would have relatives among the *Komitadji*. The Germans held the area by terrorism and bluff more than by strength of arms; they, ELAS, the Bulgars, *Komitadji*, independent Macedonians, Albanian *Ballisti* and Yugoslav partisans all used the same technique. The villages were in a quandary: on the whole, they did not love Greece, but hesitated to back Bulgaria and the Axis. They would follow whoever looked strongest.

As one of the most mixed and contested areas in the Balkans, Vitsi was fertile ground for the independent Macedonian movement. Yugoslav partisans were busily stirring up the local Slav population with propaganda, pushing the line that: 'ELAS are Fascists out for Greek territorial integrity and will oppress you. We are Communists and will liberate you.' Arrianos said the partisans were out for independent Macedonia, 'an old Bulgar trick', and that there was increased *Komitadji* activity in the area between Dendrochori and Prespa as a result. He had asked the partisans' political officer to come to Prespa to negotiate.

Arrianos's allegations were credible. After the recent night operation in Sidirochori, a *Komitadji* had sent a taunting letter: 'If you were real Allies you would wear the Red Star like the Partisans, not the national badge.' There were other signs that the Macedonian nationalist spirit was stirring; Balkan politics could break through the Resistance movement at any moment. Captain MacDonald believed that the Macedonian partisans of the second brigade and the Serbs of the first hated the Bulgars even more than the Germans. SNOF had failed to overcome the local Slavs' distrust of the Greeks. Arrianos was planning to send a platoon to Prespa, ostensibly to fight the *Komitadji*; he was 'in a queer mood of excited depression' and Pat was afraid he might be planning mischief against the Macedonian separatists.[11]

However, the real reason for Arrianos's disquiet soon became clear: ELAS divisional command wanted to transfer the Vitsi battalion to another area. Pat signalled that Arrianos and his *Andartes* were indispensable for achieving good results in NOAH'S ARK. The Vitsi detachment, he wrote later, was one of the very few units that lived up to the *Andartes'* heroic propaganda. It really was a battalion drawn from the people and as keen on fighting the foreign oppressor (the Germans) as the indigenous oppressor (anyone disliked by EAM and who could be portrayed as a grinder of the faces of the poor). Arrianos's company commanders were good fighters, whose men would follow and obey them in difficult situations.

Edmonds made strong representations to ELAS Ninth Division's leadership, but to no effect. On 21 May, without a word of farewell, Arrianos marched off towards Free Greece, taking most of his men with him. Replacement companies, consisting entirely of Greeks, not Slavs, began arriving the next day. Only about thirty local Slav *Andartes* were left in the area.

Pat was sorry to see the Vitsi detachment leave. Arrianos himself was a born political leader and natural military commander with astonishing energy and a great care for his men, who obeyed him absolutely. Arrianos and his company commanders showed a genuine warmth of feeling towards the British. Although they were thoroughly left-wing, they never hesitated to co-operate. They realized that whatever plans Great Britain might have for Greece after the war, Pat and his fellows were there to damage the Germans and were in that game up to their necks. Arrianos and his men were no angels and had murdered a few political opponents, but they 'had something cordial and genuine about them which is one of the several good things the Left-wing movement in Greece represents'. Later, Pat was proud to learn that Arrianos had good memories of him.

Giorgios Yannoulis, the new *kapetanios* of 1st Battalion, 28th Regiment ELAS, had been a lawyer in civilian life and a second lieutenant in the army reserve. He was probably the most cultivated of ELAS's commanders in Western Macedonia; it might have been supposed that he and Pat would get on, as two educated men. However, Pat was the least class-bound of Englishmen and his years in the ranks had given him a great respect and liking for the common man. He found Yannoulis 'very courteous and smooth, and thoroughly slippery'. At the outset of his ELAS career, Yannoulis had been imprisoned for two months on political grounds; now he was 'completely ELAS-minded'. In a nutshell, the two men did not get on.

Pat complained that Yannoulis's co-operation with the mission was 'great in word but almost nil in deed'[12] and the battalion's positions were now designed for fighting the *Komitadjis* rather than the Germans. While Arrianos had been keen to maintain Greek influence, he had to tread warily because most of his own *Andartes* were Slavs. The first battalion, by contrast, consisted mostly of Greeks. Company commanders were now ordered 'to prevent the advance of any enemy whatsoever, whether Germans, local reactionaries, Bulgars, *Komitadjis*, or autonomists.' Yannoulis and Lytridhis launched a campaign of harassment against the *Komitadji*, which was to last nearly the whole summer. The *Andartes* sat on the heights overlooking the armed villages and shot at anyone who came out to work in the fields; they also stole sheep and mules whenever they could. This undoubtedly worried the *Komitadji* a good deal. It also worried Pat, because it took ELAS's attention completely away from the Germans.

Yannoulis also used terror. At some time in May or June, more than twenty *Komitadjis* captured near Kastoria were brought to Yannoulis's headquarters at Vapsori and killed with knives. Two of the *Andartes* under Pat's command, who were on detachment to ELAS at the time, confessed to taking part in the slaughter. Then, in August 1944, perhaps 300 prisoners were taken in an attack on Polykeraso and Perikopi.[13] Yannoulis ordered they should be killed with knives, not shot. Pat's informant was, again, one of the killers. Mass killing with knives is a more leisurely, horrific and effective kind of terrorism than summary execution by firing squad. It is an intimate and personal kind of violence designed to make the most forceful impression on the perpetrator, on witnesses and all those nearby who fear it could happen to them.

Cairo ordered the mission to concentrate on German targets and have nothing to do with attacks against the *Komitadji*. Since moving to the woods, Pat had avoided entering any village other than Vapsori. Now he asked his agents to get him a set of civilian clothes and a German identity card. Although Pat's Greek was good enough to fool a German, any local would tell he was foreign after a short conversation. Dressed as a civilian and accompanied by 22 and 23, he would be able to move about the countryside without exciting comment.[14] When the clothes arrived, on 25 May Pat and his agents reconnoitred the Florina airfield. They noted the number and positions of the piles of ammunition, bombs and petrol as targets for demolition. Pat also had a good look at Florina from the heights immediately to the north but did not go down into the town itself for fear of being detected by one of the many local informers. There were other ways of getting intelligence. His spies were assiduous and Pat was able to build up an extensive dossier, illustrated with annotated postcards, which mapped and detailed the key German installations, facilities and billets in Florina.

Chapter Four

Special Operations

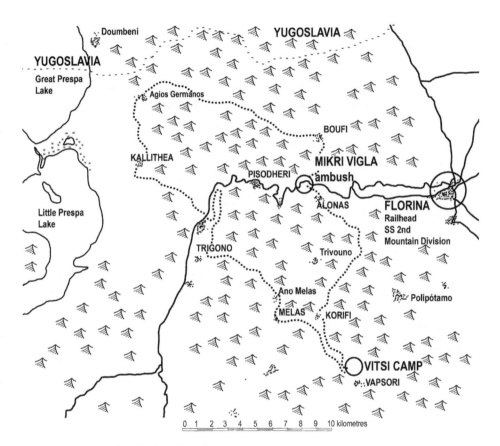

The ambush on the Florina Road.

Throughout the second half of May 1944, Pat's spies reported a stream of railway traffic bringing troops and supplies to the Florina railhead. One of the élite infantry regiments of the German First Mountain Division had gone to Albania, together with support troops, to carry out a big drive against the partisans. The road from Florina was thronged with marching troops and motorized support columns. It was time for an ambush.

On 29 May, Pat sent the commando on a leisurely march north from the camp on Mount Vitsi to a staging post at Korifi. He wanted the men to take it easy so that they would arrive fresh. They took a supply of the green, almond-smelling Nobel '808' plastic explosive, an exploder, electric detonators and cable, detonator cord and some battered anti-tank mines, as well as their rifles, Stens, hand grenades and two Italian-made Breda light machine guns. Pat had accounts to do and signals to write, which kept him in camp on Vitsi overnight. He followed in the morning with Kite, Aaron and another *Andarte*, to arrive at Korifi at noon the next day. The commando had spent the morning gathering material for a fougasse, an improvised mine dug into the rock and filled with explosives, rocks and bits of metal. The village children helped to collect a murderous assortment of old bolts, nails, hinges, spikes, horseshoes and mule shoes. Pat added some shell fragments he had found on the way from Vitsi, which would make the nose cap for the fougasse. The commando had also borrowed four spades and picks from the villagers. There would be two digging parties and it was essential to have spares; broken tools could endanger the whole operation. Kite set the commando to work connecting the anti-tank mines, so they could all be set off at once.

A platoon of *Andartes* arrived from Vapsori to join the attack. Yannoulis was meant to lead them, but had decided at the last minute that he had other urgent work and delegated the job to a former second lieutenant of the reserve with the *nom de guerre* of Souliotis. Their guide would be an *Andarte* who had been a policeman in the village of Boufi. *Andartes* and commandos set off together from Korifi at about two in the afternoon. Souliotis was in charge of the *Andarte* platoon, Pat of the commando; there was no overall commander of the whole operation. This was an unconventional arrangement, but Pat thought it would work. Souliotis would fall in with anything he said, and he did not want to command the *Andartes*. To command Greeks was hard for a Greek, harder for a foreigner, and harder still for a foreigner who did not know the particular Greeks he was commanding. If the platoon ran away when things got hot, neither Souliotis nor anyone else would be able to hold them. At the same time, Pat did not want to put the commando under Souliotis in case he wavered, as *Andarte* commanders often did. Pat was fairly sure the commandos would stand firm and had told them that, whatever the others did, they were going to see the job through to the end. *Andartes* and commandos reached the last ridge south of Alonas before sunset. The men fell out to rest while Pat, Kite, Souliotis and his second-in-command went forward to get a better view of the chosen spot.

Pat had selected a stretch 16 kilometres west of Florina at a place known locally as Mikri Vigla. Here the road was cut into the side of a tall ridge, skirting ravines and spurs as it roughly followed the contours, forming three sides of an oblong facing south, towards Alonas, with a slight bend in the middle and a high point at each end. To the west, a precipitous bluff stood above the road, thickly wooded with small beech trees; to the east, towards Florina, was a hillock thinly covered with beeches and scrub. Between the two heights stretched a col, in a curve like the cables of a suspension bridge. The dusty surface of the road showed up clearly, like a yellowish-white ribbon running along the ridge on the opposite side of the deep valley. A German column, with foot troops and horse transport, was passing.

After agreeing the layout of the explosive charges, men and weapons, and the vital line of immediate withdrawal, Pat and his companions fell out to have a smoke and wait for dark. About dusk, they started back towards Alonas. The moon was very bright and sheets of wild narcissi glistened in the dew. They moved cautiously; the Germans often used Alonas as a guard post when they were moving troops between Florina and Albania.

A shepherd boy, guarding his flocks, said there were no Germans in the village that night. When the *Andartes* told the boy that Pat was English, he rushed up, hugged and kissed him violently. Pat felt amused and slightly foolish. He thought he understood the boy's feelings, though. During the occupation, the villagers lived in a state of continual fear. The Germans commandeered food and animals, seized men for forced labour and sometimes took hostages; the *Andartes* used the village too. For the inhabitants, the occupation really was torture. Rather timidly, they looked up to anyone who resisted the Germans, whatever their nationality. England also represented the peasants' dream of a great rich nation where they might go to make a fortune that would allow them to return to live in comfort and respect. It was quite an event for an excitable Slav boy, who had never been more than 5 miles from his village, to meet two Englishmen in the middle of a summer night on the mountain.

Shepherds usually either worked in twos or threes, or kept their flocks close to one another to have company during the night. The boy left his flock in the charge of his companion and took the men down into the village. Everyone had a drink at one of the communal springs and filled their water bottles; the headman provided runners, who knew all the footpaths, to take them up to the exact point on the road.

The road was absolutely quiet. Looking east down the valley, they could see the lights of vehicles moving about in Florina, where a train had just arrived from the German army headquarters in Salonika.

They unloaded the explosives and tools from the mule and put them in the ditch, out of sight if a German column should come by during the preparations. The least reliable member of the commando was sent away to take the mule back to Vitsi.

The plan was to catch a column travelling west from Florina towards Albania; any columns moving in the opposite direction would be left alone. The ambushers would be hidden from the enemy in the thick wooded cover on the northern edge of the road. A fougasse would be dug into the steep earth bank at the side of the road and the five linked anti-tank mines dug in diagonally across the carriageway. The whole lot would be fired simultaneously.

The ambush depended on attacking from short range and taking the enemy by surprise, getting down onto the road, mopping up, collecting booty and getting away again before the Germans could do anything. They would have to seal off the selected stretch of road and cut it off from the rest of the column or any other enemy forces. One machine gun would be sited on the eastern hillock, which commanded a good stretch of road towards Florina, with the other on the bluff, so that any reinforcements would immediately come under fire. There was a remote possibility that troops from the guard post at Vigla Pisoderi, to the west, might come over the neck of the bluff to block the ambush party's retreat but this was very unlikely. Germans manning small defence posts usually rushed to their positions when they heard gunfire and waited to see what was happening. The commander would only send out a detachment when he was certain the post itself was not in danger. By then it would be too late. The post at Vigla Pisoderi was too far away and climbing over the neck of the bluff would take too long. The country north of the road, from the bluff to Boufi, consisted of a succession of thickly wooded ridges, where troops from Vigla Pisoderi would have no chance of catching the ambushers. The eastern hillock was the crucial strongpoint for the defence.

Souliotis made a quick recce. Pat checked that the machine guns would be sited close to the road and left Souliotis to put the men in position. Only Pat, Kite and six men of the commando digging party remained on the road.

Digging in the mines and explosives was difficult: the road surface was unusually good and the bank was just a half-metre layer of earth on top of impenetrable granite. It was after midnight by the time everything was in place and wired up. The fougasse and mines were invisible, but Kite very carefully took a sight on their position with Pat standing on the mines as a marker. Kite and Pat took cover in thick foliage among the roots of a beech tree, along with Aaron (who was looking after the exploder) and an *Andarte* called Vardas.

They settled down to wait. The night got very cold on the mountainside. The men talked little, in whispers, and did not move about. At dawn, they smoked a cigarette, hiding the glow behind their caps. Aaron started coughing. Pat swore at him and made him put his cigarette out.

The sun came up on another perfectly clear day. It was going to be hot.

Just before six, there was a hum of vehicles in the distance, from the direction of Florina, growing louder. 'They're coming!' Pat said. Aaron, who had fallen asleep, jumped up, grabbing his cap and his gun, rubbing his eyes and looking for the Germans. The others pulled him down again. Souliotis's *Andartes* were so well-hidden that Pat and Kite briefly wondered whether they were still there or had slipped away in the night.

Round the lower bend, at the foot of the eastern hillock, there appeared first one and then a second grey Volkswagen staff car. Kite and Pat rapidly debated whether to attack or let them pass and wait for a lorry with troops or stores. They decided to attack as staff cars were likely to contain documents.

As the leading staff car approached, Kite pressed down the plunger with his full weight of more than 13 stone. His timing was perfect. There was a sheet of flame, a roar, a cloud of dust and blackish smoke. The staff car simply vanished as the mines lifted it up in the air and the fougasse blew it over the edge.

Gunfire was coming from the wooded hillside; Pat and Kite could distinguish the different notes of the Bredas, Stens and rifles. They disconnected the exploder. Pat reeled the wire in, thrust the exploder and coil of wire into the arms of Aaron and sent him away to wait on the rear slope of the col. Vardas rushed down into the road. The car had dropped over the edge, which was almost sheer, and got caught on some sort of obstruction. The engine had been blown out; the driver was still sitting at the wheel but was not very recognizable. The German who had been sitting beside him was stumbling about with his hand to his face; he was wounded in the jaw and did not know what was happening. Vardas shot him in the head with his Sten, took his boots, pistol and a leather satchel, and climbed back up the hill.

Three Volkswagen staff cars had entered their stretch of road, which was just over 1 kilometre long. The second car had stopped a little before the halfway point; it had been shot up by a commando Breda and by Kouyias, the *kapetanios* of the commando, who was close enough to the road to get it with his Sten. There were four or five Germans in this car; two were killed outright, the others escaped down the steep hillside towards Alonas, pursued by gunfire. It was later reported that they died from their wounds in Florina hospital. As soon as they bailed out, the commando Breda turned its fire onto the third car, which had stopped at the foot of the hillock, only just inside the sealed stretch of road. The Germans jumped out and ran off.

Everything seemed to be going splendidly. There was no enemy resistance. Pat took Kite and ran full speed to the lowest point of the col, where he found a group of the commandos. He sent three of them to tip the second car over the edge and make sure it was thoroughly smashed up. Pat was pleased to see they sprinted off to do their job without any hesitation. He ordered Kite and Vardas to go to the top of the hillock and see what was happening further down the road. The light machine gun had vanished from the hillock. Pat himself took another commando, Zoutas, and ran full speed down the road to the third car. The radiator was shot up but there did not appear to be any other damage. He wanted to push the car over the edge, but there was a dry-stone wall on the outer side of the road at that point; they would have to push the car about 25 metres further west to reach a place where they could send it over the edge. Unfortunately, there was a slight up-gradient and it was very hard to shift the car. Zoutas wanted to put a sticky bomb on the engine but Pat stopped him. Pat tried to get into the car to drive it up the road but, in a moment of farce, he got in on the nearer right-hand side and couldn't get past the handbrake and gear lever to the driving seat. He had just got out again to go round to the driver's door when he realized that he was alone in the road. Zoutas was well away, making for the col. Kite and Vardas were running down from the hillock, shouting and beckoning. He couldn't hear a word they said, but Kite would not be pulling out unless he had a very good reason.

Pat would be an easy target for any Germans who might come round the corner. He grabbed two large briefcases, released the handbrake and gave the car a good shove before running up the road as fast as he could towards the col.

The bank was 3 metres sheer, all smooth earth without a foothold. Completely out of breath and weighed down by the heavy briefcases, Pat knew he couldn't get up it by taking a run. A little further on, the bank was slightly lower. Pat tried to get up, but fell. He succeeded at the second attempt but was so exhausted that he couldn't move. Fortunately no Germans appeared. After lying there for perhaps twenty seconds, he got up and scrambled along to the col where he found Kite, Souliotis, Vardas, Aaron and several commandos.

Kite reported that on reaching the top of the hillock he had come under fire. The German column of trucks stretched so far down the road that he could not see the end of it. Troops had dismounted and got to the top of the next hillock. Overall, though, things were going very well. They had held the road for thirty-five minutes; they had the briefcases and other booty from the staff cars.

Half a kilometre away, they got into dead ground among dense beech scrub. There they stopped and pooled the haul, which included a large sack of personal mail, parcels and newspapers, and several briefcases full of documents. They kept all the documents, letters and parcels; Pat took one copy of each newspaper and dumped the rest. Further on, when almost all the commando had regrouped along with a few of Souliotis's *Andartes*, they divided up the sugar, biscuits, cake (from Vienna) and cigarettes. There were also some very good haversack rations that had belonged to *Hauptmann* Xavier Fuss, a staff officer killed in the ambush. They did not save anything for the absentees, who had pulled out too quickly. Not one of Souliotis's party had gone down on to the road, and his light machine-gun team had left Pat in the lurch. If it had held its position, the Germans would have had to take cover instead of being able to make for the high ground and defend themselves, and Pat should have been able to destroy the third car completely. The job had really been done by the commandos: nearly all of them had done well and the machine-gunner who shot up the second car, a youth called Poulis with a slow smile and very few words, had been outstanding. Kite had nicknamed him 'Moe' (after one of the 'Three Stooges' comedy team), but he was far from stupid, an excellent shot and very cool.

Now, they had to get away. The rest of 31 May was spent dodging about among the wooded ridges near Boufi, collecting up the members of the band until nearly everyone was there. It was extremely hot and they were all feeling the lack of sleep.

There was an argument about where to go next. The *Andartes* were full of confidence after the successful ambush. Most of them wanted to go into Boufi and bed down in the village. Pat and Kite were against the idea: the Germans would probably go there to arrest people for interrogation. There was also the question of when, and by what route, they should go back across the main road to return to Vitsi. Souliotis wanted to go that night, by way of Alonas. Pat was against this too: the Germans would probably occupy Alonas for a few days and Pat did not want them to know that the ambushers had come from Vitsi. It would be better if the enemy thought the attack had come from Boufi, Prespa or somewhere north of the Yugoslav border. He wanted to keep Vitsi secure as a base for NOAH'S ARK. However, he also wanted to get away from the scene of the ambush before the Germans came searching.

Souliotis finally agreed that they should lie up in the woods outside Boufi and only enter the village after sunset to collect rations, having first sent in a civilian to see that everything was all right. Then they should march by night to Prespa, where Pat hoped to contact Deyan and his partisans.

About midday, when they were relaxing in a small plantation of larches, twenty minutes out of Boufi, there was a shout: 'The Germans are coming!' Everyone got up and fled in a mad rush. An *Andarte* ran into Pat, knocking him over in his haste. Kite and Pat had to follow or be left in the lurch. Everyone kept looking behind but no one could see any Germans. After moving fast for some minutes, first through a bog and then uphill through dense thickets, Kite and Pat had had enough; if there were any Germans in pursuit, this would be a good place for a shoot. Some of the commando, at least, had stayed with them while the rest went streaming on with the *Andartes*. (Souliotis was somewhere at the head of the rush; Pat did not see him again until they got back to Vapsori, days later.)

The landscape was peaceful. There was not a German in sight.

According to Mavros, the officer in charge of the *Andarte* machine gun who had gone to ground outside Boufi, a few Germans had approached the village. It looked as if they didn't even know about the ambush. They were just there to grab some food and take a couple of mules and labourers for a job in Florina. The *Andartes* had kept their heads down and the Germans had not seen them.

While waiting to go down into Boufi, Pat had a look at the captured documents. It was clear he had got hold of something important. There was a list of the code-names of all the units of the First Mountain Division, due to come into force the next day, which would give British Intelligence a complete picture of the division. There was also information about higher formations, administration and training in the German army, a telegram from Army Group F to the Mountain Division about the drive, code-name *Einhorn*, and a list of promotions 'signed by Adolf himself'.

At nightfall, the group got food and runners from Boufi and set off over the mountains toward Agios Germanos, which lies at the foot of the mountains, at the eastern end of the shingle isthmus dividing the two Prespa lakes.

It was a gruelling march, through lovely but inhospitable country. The confused mass of Mount Varnous lay between Boufi and their destination. Getting to Agios Germanos would mean crossing a high watershed at over 1,900 metres, a good 900 metres above Boufi. They struggled through a snowfield 1 metre deep, glistening in the moonlight, on a tract of jagged boulders. Despite the cold, the men sweated and suffered from thirst before they came to a spring near the divide.

Shambling along, hardly able to walk any more, Kite and Pat agreed that they were enjoying themselves immensely.

As the men neared Agios Germanos at about five in the morning, it was obvious that some of the commandos were nearly finished. The village had become a promised land, a place to get food and sleep.

Agios Germanos looked enticing, with a large church, tall shady trees, brilliant grass, peaceful orchards and a clear trout stream tumbling down into the lake from the divide between two great bluffs. Some way beyond the village, Great Prespa Lake gleamed a soft pale blue in the early-morning light. Beyond that stood the grey and pink mountains of Albania, barren and magnificent. Everyone relaxed in the village square. Vardas, who had been something of a brigand chief in Prespa, had a long conversation with the village headman, an evil-looking old fellow with charming manners and a clownish sense of comedy. The Slav villagers were generally friendly to the partisans, more or less friendly to ELAS, and on the whole did not like the Bulgarians. Inevitably, though, there were a few pro-Bulgars, one of whom had slipped away the night before. During the night, a loyal peasant had come with a warning that the Bulgarians were expected to send down a detachment from the garrison at Doumbeni later in the day. Deyan's partisans had taken to the hills and Pat's commando had to get away.

The road skirting the east bank of Little Prespa was too exposed to Bulgarian forces with motorized transport. They must go the hard way and take the goat tracks across the mountain, up and down, over deep eroded ravines of shale. It was a hot morning, there was no water and the commandos were suffering. Their *kapetanios* said: 'They are dying standing up! They can go no further!' Pat said they had to, and walked on with Kite, Vardas and Aaron. Reluctantly, the commando trailed behind. Eventually they reached the little village of Kallithea, just 4 kilometres to the south, and settled down for the day. Everyone collapsed in the churchyard, under the trees, sleeping on tombs. The villagers were frightened. At one time or another they had suffered from the Bulgars, the Germans, ELAS, Yugoslav partisans, Albanian partisans and marauding bands of independent Macedonians. It took an effort to persuade them that the British and the commandos were not hostile and would pay for food. Then the villagers were very good to their unexpected visitors. One came round with a large iron pot full of sour milk, 'which is probably the most refreshing drink in the world for a hot day. The men just roused themselves enough for him to ladle a little into their mouths, and then dropped back as if the refreshing liquid had killed them.'

Kite and Pat lay awake in the cloister along the side of the church. They were both very jumpy; if the Bulgars came and took the party by surprise, things would not go well. Even when fresh, the *Andartes* were unsteady in defence. Now the men were exhausted, entirely given over to sleep. Pat had posted sentries at vantage points outside the village and changed them every hour. He and Kite had to drag the men to their feet to wake them up when it was their turn.

Pat, Kite, Vardas, Aaron, Mavros and the ex-policeman ate an excellent meal, starting with several glasses of *tsipouro*, followed by an omelette with a good white wine, black bread and white cheese, and pints of strong tea to finish. During the meal, Vardas (as an expert on Prespa) had a violent quarrel with their official guide (who had never been there) about the best route for re-crossing the main road once it was dark.

March discipline was essential for moving on foot through hostile country. Mavros got all the *Andartes* on parade and gave them a harangue. Kite and Pat had not had more than an hour's sleep since leaving Vitsi, more than sixty hours earlier; they were in no fit state for the long march back across the mountain ridges. Before moving off, they each took a benzedrine tablet from Kite's escape kit.

With the help of runners from Kallithea, the party crossed the road safely. Now the official guide took over and led them through a dense beech forest, tangled with undergrowth and without a track.

He was soon lost. First he took them much too far to the left, almost to the Vigla guard post, then much too far to the right, almost into the village of Trigonon. Here, in the woods where no one could see them, on the morning of 2 June Pat told the commando they could make fires and bed down. He, though, was in a hurry to get back to the radio set. With Kite, Vardas and Aaron (who was still faithfully carrying the exploder), Pat took all the documents and made for Melas. There they hired four animals to ride, very slowly, back to base, falling asleep in the saddle before finally reaching the camp on Vitsi in time for tea.

The next day, Kite set out with Aaron for Pendalofos to deliver the captured documents to Captain Wickstead, before they were sent out of the country. A few weeks later, a signal came expressing the Director of Military Intelligence's appreciation.[1]

Pat wrote that it had been 'a successful op and the most enjoyable trip of my life'. It was a good example of what a special operation was meant to do: they had discomforted the enemy, given a much larger force a bloody nose, and captured high-quality intelligence. The German response had been feeble. Rather than pursue their attackers, they had sent an infantry detachment to the col, where they had thrown a couple of hand grenades into the bushes as a gesture, without even leaving the road to search the woods. They arrested six or seven villagers in Alonas, but released them the same evening. The next morning, German troops brought six hostages from Florina and hanged them on the beech trees among the ambush positions, as an example. Months later, Pat discovered that the hanged men not only had nothing to do with the ambush, they were not even from Alonas but came from Florina jail, where they had been under arrest for some time.

Even in midsummer, camping out on Mount Vitsi was cold and uncomfortable; there were still frequent torrents of rain or hail on the mountain in June and once a snowstorm. However, the group was healthy and the camp was clean. Pat always told his men to eat, drink and be merry because no one knew what tomorrow might bring; after the raid, he laid on a great feast with roasted lambs to celebrate their success.[2] Although it was still difficult to get eggs, milk and meat, June had brought strawberries and cream in 'quantities beyond the dreams of gluttony'. It was a patriotic duty to eat as much as humanly possible to stop the strawberry crop reaching Florina and being sold to the Germans. Stiff cream was the cheapest form of fat, less than half the price of butter. Delivered in petrol tins, it was so rich that it was impossible to eat much at a time.

Pat was busy gathering intelligence. On 8 June Wickstead sent Cairo a summary of Pat's information about the movement of the First Mountain Division, which gives a good idea of the details and quality of the reports:

From 24 May to 1 June there arrived at Florina from the north 20 trains 670 wagons containing 5790 tps 238 MT 240 horses 15 ATK quantity 75 mm incl 1 train ammo. A big percentage of the men and guns are mountain. From 24 May to 3 June there passed from Florina to the West 6800 tps on foot and 229 MT. These figures are conservative and not a complete record. Before the ambush the movement was copious from dusk to dawn. It stopped on 1 June and started again on 2 June. A big percentage of Poles Ities etc. Transit camp 6067 and 6264. A report states that officers and ORs from Florina are said to have come from Montenegro to Ithaca Corfu Cephalonia. 2 from ELAS.... A conference was held at Ioannina on 27 May between Lanz [GOC 22nd Army Corps] and the commanders from Agrinion and Belgrade. (*Generalleutnant*) Stettner was probably in Belgrade just before 27 May.[3]

Pat as a young man, c.1936, from his family photo album.

Jill (Julia) Rendel on her 29th birthday, 12 May 1942, from Pat's family photo album.

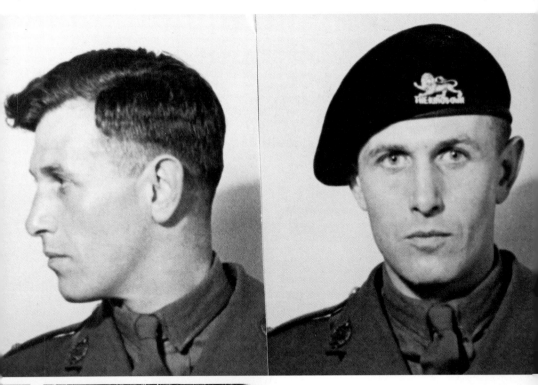

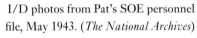
I/D photos from Pat's SOE personnel file, May 1943. (*The National Archives*)

Lieutenant Colonel Nick Hammond: I/D photo from his SOE personnel file in The National Archives (taken before he grew his famous moustaches in Greece).

Pat's parachute release buckle.

Boodle headquarters,
Pendalofos, photographed by
the author in 2013.

Captain (later Major) Ronald Prentice, from his SOE personnel file. (*The National Archives*)

ELAS Ninth Division commanders, 1944. The *kapetanios* Karatsas (Ieronimos Troianos) is seated fourth from right, wearing spectacles; seated next to him in the centre of the picture is Aggelos Blahopoulos, a former major in the regular army, who was at the time *stratiotikos* (military commander) of the Ninth Division. Rennos Michaleas, the *politikos*, is provisionally identified as the man third from left in the middle row. (*Courtesy of Penelopi Bliakga*)

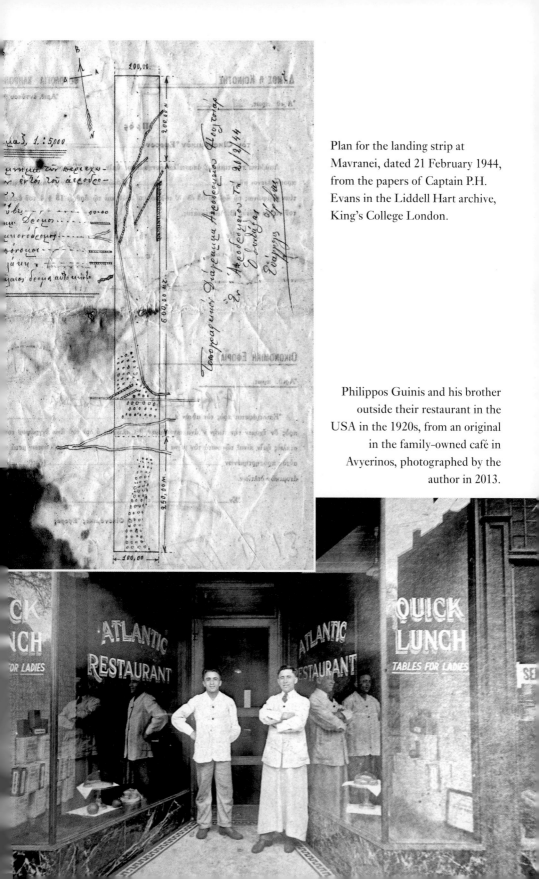

Plan for the landing strip at Mavranei, dated 21 February 1944, from the papers of Captain P.H. Evans in the Liddell Hart archive, King's College London.

Philippos Guinis and his brother outside their restaurant in the USA in the 1920s, from an original in the family-owned café in Avyerinos, photographed by the author in 2013.

Vapsori as it was in 1944, from a ceramic plaque on the church photographed by the author in 2010.

Mount Vitsi from the north, photographed by the author.

A group of *Andartes*, Vapsori 1944, from Pat's family photo album.

Western Macedonian *Andarte* leaders, 1944. Arrianos – founder and leader of the Vitsi battalion – is fourth from left. (*Courtesy of Penelopi Bliakga*)

Collecting munitions: an SOE RAF sergeant with a group of *Andartes*, August 1944. The drums in front of the group are parachute container cells (several of which fitted together inside a container), from Pat's family photo album.

'Fertiliser': the camp on Mount Vitsi, May 1944, from Pat's family photo album.

Florina targets, 1944: a postcard marked up by Pat's spies to show buildings occupied by German forces, from the papers of Captain P.H. Evans in the Liddell Hart archive, King's College London.

Captain Pat Evans in Western Macedonia, 1944, from Pat's family photo album.

Little Prespa Lake, photographed by the author.

Great Prespa Lake, photographed by the author.

Mission accomplished! Members of Force 133 in Kozani on their way to leave Greece via Salonika, November 1944, from Pat's family photo album.

Captain Geoffrey Chandler, Florina, summer 1945, from Pat's family photo album.

AGIS on Mount Vermion, 1945; Pat and Geoffrey Chandler on the left, from Pat's family photo album.

Pat and Geoffrey Chandler (kneeling, centre) on patrol with AGIS in the Florina district, summer 1945, from Pat's family photo album.

Kastoria, June 1945: opening a new AGIS Information Centre, with the mayor in a white suit and the bishop, from Pat's family photo album.

Florina market, 1945, from Pat's family photo album.

Silver filigree bracelet: 'From Nat Pilides: To my dear Captain P.H. Evans' in December 1945, photographed by the author.

Egyptian scarab, brought back by Pat from Cairo.

Political rally with girls in traditional costume, Florina 1945, from Pat's family photo album.

Jill, Pat and Tommy, Hampstead, summer 1950, from Pat's family photo album.

Former muleteer Christos Dalamitros, aged 95, photographed by the author in Florina, 2010.

Vapsori church, 2010, photographed by the author.

The ruins of Vapsori, 2010, photographed by the author.

German troops were constantly on the move and a new guard post had been established at the site of the ambush. An order was issued by the authorities in Florina and Kastoria forbidding any civilians, *Komitadjis* included, to go out of their villages on pain of death. Having finished its big drive in Albania, the First Mountain Division was beginning to prepare something else. Lytridhis and Yannoulis were hardly even pretending to resist the Germans now. Whenever Pat insisted that action against the Germans was necessary, they said yes, they fully realized; no one regretted more than they, but they could do nothing just then. The excuse was always the *Komitadjis*. Pat thought this was nonsense; there were no *Komitadjis* to the north, east or west, only to the south. Lytridhis and Yannoulis were full of flowery courtesy, took the sovereigns and gave no practical co-operation in return. Relations grew so bad that Pat delivered an ultimatum. Lieutenant Colonel Edmonds would have to decide whether to continue supporting ELAS on Vitsi.

On 11 June, Edmonds arrived from Pendalofos with his interpreter. On the way up, they had passed through Dendrochori, where Edmonds asked Yannoulis if he had any troops nearby and if anything was happening. Yannoulis said no, all the *Andartes* were in their positions on Vitsi. Edmonds knew this was untrue and said so: Yannoulis had three companies just to the north, on Mount Mali Madhi, where they were surrounding a Free Macedonian band led by a villager called Peyo, who came from Gavros. Yannoulis had been covered with confusion. Now, on Vitsi, it was Lytridhis's turn to look uncomfortable. Finally it was agreed that Pat would carry on supporting the battalion. After climbing to the top of Mount Vitsi to look at the lie of the land, Edmonds and his interpreter went back to Pendalofos.

Pat was briefly joined by Major Scott, the engineer officer in charge of demolitions in Greece, who had come to reconnoitre the Klidhi railway bridge with Pat and work out the explosive requirements for NOAH'S ARK. Scott saw that the defences were too strong to allow the *Andartes* to capture and hold the bridge while a sapper party carried out the demolition, and an attacking force could easily be cut off from the flanks. Instead, he came up with another plan. After experimenting with buried charges, he devised a way of blowing up the railway with mined charges laid in unguarded stretches of the line, fitted with booby-traps and set off by 'L-delay' fuses set for various different times. The fuse was a kind of pencil switch with a timing device that combined a spring and a lead link. When it was set, the tension of the spring gradually stretched the lead until it broke and released the firing pin. Switches came in boxes of ten with different delays, ranging from an hour to twenty-eight days, at 65°F. There was a considerable margin of error in the timing, but the switches were otherwise reliable, small and silent.

Scott and Pat discussed other possible operations on the roads running through Florina to Monastir in Yugoslavia to the north and Albania in the west. One plan involved a series of fougasses and mined charges, aimed at a column of infantry; another was for an ambush, with small-arms fire rather than explosives. There was a good site on the road near Vatochori, the next village north of Gavros, but an attack there would attract a German drive on Vitsi. Pat preferred a more distant stretch between Kristalopiyi and Kapetista, preferably on the Albanian side of the frontier, where an ambush might draw off some of the German forces attacking the partisans.

On the afternoon of 16 June, one half of the commando left (taking mines, sticky bombs, and explosives) to spend the night at Dendrochori with a section of *Andartes*. At seven o'clock the next morning, Germans from Kastoria and eighty *Komitadjis* entered the village. The *Andartes* had only posted one sentry, who had fallen asleep; they were taken completely by surprise. The attackers killed eleven *Andartes*, including three of Pat's commandos. Three other commandos were wounded, several civilians were killed and some mules and horses taken.

Pat arrived at 2200 hours that evening with Major Scott, Kite and the second section of the commando, knowing nothing of the disaster. Piecing together eyewitness accounts, he established that one of his commandos, Kouyias, had been wounded, captured and put to death by the *Komitadjis* with an axe. Another, Gavanas, had been killed outright in the fighting. The third, Paskhos, had been in one of the houses that were set alight to force the *Andartes* into the open. He had not come out. A shot had been heard from inside the blazing house and it was presumed he had killed himself. All that was found of his body was a charred stump. The dead commandos had all put up a stiff resistance, but some of the others had run away without their weapons or even their boots.

Scott rode back to Pendalofos; Kite and Pat to Vitsi. The wounded were put on mules and brought back with the remaining men. Kite went on to the camp while Pat stayed in Vapsori to interrogate two young German privates who had deserted from an SS artillery company. They were not fanatical Nazis, just ordinary lads. The interrogation went well and, at Pat's direction, they wrote a letter to their comrades encouraging them, too, to desert. Sixteen did, although two were later recaptured. After promising that they would be properly treated as PoWs, ELAS took the two prisoners south to Free Greece, where they were murdered a few weeks later. Pat believed that many German privates (though not officers or NCOs) were ready to desert, but were held back by fear of being taken prisoner by the *Andartes*, tortured, mutilated and killed. Their fear was partly justified; the *Andartes'* treatment of prisoners was in turn partly justified by the German policy of shooting captured *Andartes* out of hand.

Three days later, on 21 June, the commando, Kite and Pat left the camp to try again. They had arranged with Lytridhis to meet up with nine sections of ELAS Andartes (about 100 men), with a considerable number of machine guns, at the village of Ieropiyi. Most of the following night was spent in ambush where the road from Florina to Albania crossed the frontier through a steep, narrow defile. It was not perhaps the ideal spot, but good enough.

The commando took up positions about 150 yards from the road, with a long, steep slope behind them. 'Moe' settled down with his light machine gun and dug himself in, as calm and phlegmatic as usual. The commandos' job was to halt the leading vehicle and, if possible, shoot up the second one as well, leaving ELAS to deal with the rest of the column. However, the *Andartes* would not come down near to the road alongside the commando but stayed above them, near the top of the defile. This would not only make the *Andartes* less effective but created a terrible risk that they might fire on commandos by mistake in the confusion. When a column passed in the dark, Pat would not allow anyone to open fire; rather than risk a shambles, he waited to catch another column at dawn or in the first two hours of daylight.

None came. The RAF had recently taken to flying sorties of twin-engined Beaufighters from Italy, to such good effect that the Germans had become reluctant to move large columns by daylight.

Back the commando went, from the ambush site to their camp, where they were reinforced by a column of mules bringing food, mail and cigarettes, two Poles and two Czechs, and a Greek cook. The *Andartes* had dug up the road along the Aliakmon; now a German infantry battalion started clearing it, moving south from Vatochori to Kastoria, leaving guard posts and patrols behind them. At the same time a large concentration of troops was gathering in Florina and the villages of the Florina plain. It looked as if the enemy was preparing an assault on Vitsi.

The camp had moved to a new position on the main peak, on the edge of dense, precipitous woods. Pat decided to sit tight until the situation crystallized. Nothing much seemed to be happening, so Pat and Kite went down into Vapsori to see Lytridhis and prepare an ambush attempt at Gavros. Lytridhis, though, had news. Some 500 Germans had arrived at the crossroads just south of Gavros with mortars, machine guns and a truck of dogs. They had established a guard post and sent out patrols: Fertiliser must move immediately.

Kite and Pat returned to camp at midnight, roused everybody and set to work packing up. All the explosives had been cached in a deep pit in the woods, roofed with timber, thatched with straw and covered with earth and leaves, so they could move out quickly. The station would move en bloc to Prespa, which was of no significance to the Germans but close enough to Vitsi for Pat to keep an eye on the situation and carry out further operations when the chance arose.

At seven-thirty on the morning of 1 July, the party set out. For the first hour, a Heinkel circled round at about 2,000ft above the summit of Vitsi. The Germans had used aircraft in the same way at the beginning of the big drive on Mount Vermion and it looked as if Vitsi was to be the theatre of another.

At Korifi, Pat paused to meet the political commissar of the Second Macedonian Brigade of the Yugoslav partisans. The mission and commando then travelled non-stop, except for short halts every two hours, to camp outside Kallithea. The Greek members of the party thought this was a very unsafe place as there was a German guard post the other side of the ridge at Antartiko and a Bulgar garrison over the border to the north at Doumbeni. Pat reckoned it was long odds against being discovered by either and the only danger lay in betrayal. Before moving further, he sent Vardas and Aaron (the oldest, steadiest and wiliest Greeks in the group) to see what food they would be able to get on the other side of Little Prespa Lake, and whether there would be any interference from the Albanian *Ballisti*. While he was waiting, Pat met the Yugoslav partisan commander Deyan, who was on his way to Vitsi to calm down the trouble caused by the Peyo incident, which had stirred up anti-Greek feeling among the Slav Macedonian villagers. After a week camped near Kallithea, Fertiliser moved to a site near Pili, a hospitable Greek refugee village on the west bank of Little Prespa. Here they made camp.

The weather was hot and, to boost morale, Pat sent two men over the border into Albania to buy beer. When they got back, they put the beer in the lake to cool. Suddenly, with a tremendous popping, the bottles started to explode; thinking they were coming under attack, the men panicked and ran to hide.[4]

July proved to be an interesting but uneventful month as far as Fertiliser was concerned. The drive was not aimed at Vitsi after all, but at Pendalofos. The whole of the Vitsi battalion went south to Free Greece to help ELAS 28 Regiment. One platoon, which was attached to the battalion but not part of it, was sent to maintain ELAS influence in the Prespa villages, where the Macedonians looked on it as a Greek occupying force.

With the Germans and the Vitsi battalion busy with Pendalofos, operations were out of the question. Life would have been pleasant by the lake were it not for the mosquitoes that bred in the marshes and carried malaria. Pat made two trips back to Vitsi, using a house in Korifi as his base. He briefed his agents and collected their information, resulting in an RAF bombing raid on Florina on 28 July, which put the railway station out of action for more than a fortnight. He conferred with Lytridhis, who had stayed behind while Yannoulis commanded the battalion down in Free Greece. He took explosives from the Vitsi dump and made two smaller dumps near Alonas in preparation for NOAH'S ARK, and bought supplies of wheat and barley as a reserve against Fertiliser's return.

By the end of July, Pat concluded that trying to do both liaison and commando work was more than he could manage. He needed another officer and at least one interpreter. One liaison officer was needed to work with ELAS and another to keep the commando busy with operations to stop them from getting slack. With no interpreter, whenever there were discussions with ELAS, an agent's report to translate, or some haggling over the price of meat, Pat had to do it himself. On top of all this, he had the duties of a station commander with thirty people to manage and provide for. He was doing three men's work and Kite's excellent abilities were being wasted because of the language obstacle. Depressed and weary, Pat asked to go to Pendalofos and sort things out, leaving Kite in charge.

Chapter Five

NOAH'S ARK

While Fertiliser was camped out of harm's way by Little Prespa, the three divisions of the German 22 Army Corps swept through the North Pindus Mountains and 'Free Greece'. The ELAS Ninth Division left Pindus en masse, in a hurry, for the distant safety of the Pieria; the mission and Raiding Support Regiment evacuated Pendalofos, broke up into small groups and scattered into the surrounding mountains with the Germans in hot pursuit.

When the drive was over, the scattered British forces regrouped at Pendalofos and counted the damage. All the mission staff were safe, although the Germans had captured three RSR soldiers and a wireless operator. As usual, the Greek population had borne the brunt of the suffering. Boodle signalled to Cairo that the Germans had taken 300 captive civilians, 50 *Andartes* and 5 girl *Andartes* to Ioannina, with 2,000 mules and horses, and 10,000 sheep and goats. Some 300 Italians, an unknown number of civilians and *Andartes*, 1,000 mules and horses, and 5,000 to 10,000 sheep and goats were taken to Argos Orestikon. Boodle estimated that 160 villages and 3,000 houses had been burned. The villagers welcomed the mission back warmly but were furious with ELAS, which had not protected them and now returned to re-impose itself with terror and summary justice.

From the military perspective, the damage lay in the loss of matériel and the harm done to relations between the Special Forces and ELAS. The British had lost three of their four anti-tank guns and two mortars, enormous quantities of ammunition and tons of explosives. Relations between ELAS and the mission were as bad as they had ever been: ELAS had ordered the AMM to concentrate in Pendalofos and had stolen ammunition and explosives from several dumps.

Relations between the Raiding Support Regiment and ELAS were even worse. The RSR was there to support the *Andartes* with heavy weapons. However, apart from one small engagement at Eptachori, there had been no ELAS to support: the *Andartes* had simply disappeared before the enemy got close. ELAS now went so far as to arrest several RSR personnel, impose travel restrictions and demand that the RSR should stay together under *Andarte* guard.

Major Astell recommended that the RSR should be withdrawn altogether and left for Italy. Edmonds also sent a withdrawal plan for London's consideration.

Woodhouse (commanding officer, but still away from Greece) and Hammond (acting commander on the ground) both recommended that the mission and RSR should stay put. Withdrawal would be dangerous and there was still a chance to mend relations with ELAS. However, it was clear that operational plans would have to be rethought: as a result of the drive and losses, it would be weeks before the SOE and the RSR could possibly be ready. German withdrawal could begin at any moment and what would ELAS do then?

Eggs moved Edmonds south to his headquarters to act as chief liaison with ELAS, giving Prentice operational command of SOE mission operations in Western Macedonia. Given his head, Prentice proved to be a strong leader and took a hard line. He demanded and got from General Sarafis (the overall military commander of ELAS) the dismissal of Karayiannis and a reorganization of Ninth Division *stratigio*.

Pat arrived back in Pendalofos at the beginning of August 1944 to an atmosphere of intense activity. The mission was furiously busy, negotiating with ELAS, working out new tactics and targets for NOAH'S ARK, organizing replacements for lost weapons (the anti-tank guns would be replaced with Browning heavy machine guns) and arranging food and ammunition dumps.

Pat contributed a report designed to give headquarters a better understanding of Vitsi: it was a 'strategic little area' offering plenty of opportunities for attack in NOAH'S ARK but it was vulnerable to countermeasures and could be quickly overrun by a German drive.[1] SOE and RSR forces should, he suggested, be divided into small parties of between two and five men; these could move and hide easily, and would change position every few days. Even if the enemy made a drive, he would not know where to find them. The small parties could carry out minor guerrilla operations by themselves or reassemble to carry out larger operations.

They would have to take care of the local political and ethnic divisions, and there would always be some risk of betrayal: the enemy in Florina sometimes got intelligence of mission and *Andarte* positions in Vitsi, either by force from civilians buying supplies or volunteered by locals with pro-Bulgar sympathies. Even in friendly villages there was always the chance of an informer who would give them away to the Germans. On the whole, people were well-disposed to the Allies but distrustful: most of the Slav Macedonians believed that Britain wanted to restore the King of Hellenes, and the king to them meant Metaxas. Metaxas had banned the Macedonians from speaking their Slav language in public and outlawed the keeping of goats (to prevent damage to the forests). He enforced the bans with doses of castor oil (a powerful laxative, resulting in uncontrollable diarrhoea), fines, imprisonment or even banishment to Bulgaria. It was important to make a good impression in Slav villages and allay the villagers' suspicions, and to stress that the

Allies wanted everybody to be able to vote freely, after the war, for whatever regime they wanted.

Although the Slavs were a minority in Greece, they were the majority on Mount Vitsi. Almost half the women and a few of the old men spoke little or no Greek. Generally, the population disliked, distrusted and feared the Greeks. EAM, 'dressed up in pseudo-Macedonian guise, as SNOF' had gone a little way to reducing the suspicion but not very far. ELAS was tolerated and supported (rather grudgingly) partly because the villagers knew that they might be bullied if they did not provide runners, food and lodging, and partly because Macedonian national feeling was sluggish and smouldering rather than an active independence movement. A couple of villages (Asprogia and Drosopigi) spoke a good deal of Albanian, another (Agios Andonios) was a refugee village and spoke Turkish, and there were a few Vlachs, but none of these constituted a political or military problem. Pat emphasized:

> It is an unusually Balkan piece of the Balkans. In Triandafilia I once spent an hour or so in a house belonging to a family of proved Allied sympathies; on calling attention to a 'Greater Bulgaria' map on the wall (on the lines of 'Greater Germany' maps prepared by the Nazis before the war), I was told: 'Oh yes, that was put up by the father of the family who has run away to Florina and is working in the Bulgar propaganda office there.' ... *Andartes* who take part in ELAS operations against *Komitadji* villages in some cases come from *Komitadji* villages themselves, and so on.

If Greeks and Slavs wanted to cut each other's throats after the war, that would be their own affair. Fortunately, both ELAS and the partisans agreed that friction over Macedonian independence should be discouraged until the war was over. Rennos, as *politikos* of the Ninth Division, and his opposite number from 2 Brigade of Yugoslav partisans had been going round the Vitsi villages saying that it was not the time for disputes about the future of Macedonia.

Pat's report landed on the desk of Major Boxshall at SOE in London, who forwarded it on 6 September to the Foreign Office Southern Europe desk, with a comment that: 'It contains some interesting information on the extraordinary mixture of populations in that part of Greece, which might be of value to your historical section or that concerned with drawing up future boundaries.' This hardly suggested urgency. A month later, an official noted on the file: 'I am sorry to have held this up. An interesting report. Foreign Office Research Department to see.' No more was heard of it.

In Pendalofos, Pat received mail from Jill, but pressure of work prevented him from scribbling more than a note back and even this got delayed:

10 August 1944 – mixed up and sent on 24

My darling Jill,

I just got your letters dated 13 July. As usual they were very welcome. I have a rush of work and can't write you anything worth reading. Could you send me some books? Or rather, buy one – *Ha! Ha! Among the Trumpets* by Alun Lewis – and keep it for me, and buy one and send it to me? The *Maximes et Réflexions* of La Rochefoucauld. The edition I would prefer is the Jouaust if it's easily available. And do you think you could send me some English cigarettes? Nothing superlative, just the ordinary gasper. I believe you can get them sent duty free by Rothmans.

As for myself, I am well; very browned off with the war; homesick; I could sit in the middle of the floor and cry. Darling, write me one of your beautiful letters about the latest village doings, and tell me to snap out of it. My one and only aim in life is to get back to England, lead you firmly off to marry me and settle down in a house of our own – from which nothing but dynamite will ever shift us.

Up until this point, headquarters in Cairo had broadly followed the policy set by its commanding officer on the ground. Eggs, who was now based some 80 miles south of Pendalofos, in close liaison with ELAS headquarters, was convinced that the communist and ELAS leadership were mainly interested in building up forces, food, gold and weapons to seize power after the Germans left. He did not believe that ELAS had the will or the ability to attack the German withdrawal. NOAH'S ARK would have to depend on small groups of the Raiding Support Regiment and its American equivalent, with support from the liaison officers and specially-selected *Andartes* known as *Closandartes*. Eggs planned to direct NOAH'S ARK operations on the ground, leaving Edmonds to liaise with ELAS headquarters and Prentice to run Western Macedonia. However, the War Office disagreed and Cairo chose this moment to intervene. A senior regular officer, Brigadier Barker-Benfield, arrived at Eggs' headquarters to make his own assessment of ELAS. He quickly decided that the military commander, General Sarafis, was a kindred spirit, a smart and professional soldier who would fight the Germans with determination and vigour. ELAS would be given more arms and ammunition; Barker-Benfield himself would direct NOAH'S ARK from Cairo, as a straightforward military operation, conducted by ELAS with British and American Special Forces in a subordinate, supporting role.

Eggs disagreed strongly, argued and was overruled. He resigned his command and left Greece on 29 August.[2]

Pat returned to his station on Mount Vitsi. An interpreter, Gerry Livieratos, had travelled up to join Kite while Pat was on his way down to Pendalofos; another liaison officer, Captain Collins, had arrived and more were on their way. Pat had the reinforcements he wanted. Even ELAS was showing signs of activity against the Germans: on 2 September, Prentice signalled to say that the *Andartes* had occupied Siatista, Argos Orestikon and Kastoria and claimed to have ambushed the withdrawing Huns.

The order 'Smashem' was relayed to Pat on 5 September: NOAH'S ARK would start with a co-ordinated series of attacks on 8 September.

Early in the morning, Collins, Kite and the commando destroyed 200 metres of railway line in the Klidhi Pass, cutting the artery to Yugoslavia to the north; they laid three delayed crater charges along the tracks and mined the road through the pass. Collins reported that the expected ELAS *Andartes* had not turned up to take part in the attack on the railway. Pat, with a section of the Raiding Support Regiment and a platoon of *Closandartes*, blew the Albania-Florina road.

Almost nightly actions followed: mining of roads, blowing of bridges, railways and culverts (and blowing them again after they were repaired), harassment of enemy guard posts and occasionally a larger-scale ambush. Within a few days, two more sections of RSR arrived and Fertiliser was strengthened by two more officers, Captain Tozer and Lieutenant Dutton, who had landed by DC3 at the Mavranei airfield before travelling to Vapsori to join Fertiliser. Tozer took charge of the substation Pat had established at Boufi to support attacks on the Albania-Florina road.[3] In the middle of October, a patrol from the Long Range Desert Group under the command of the splendidly-named Major Stormonth-Darling came to work with them, having parachuted in to Argos Orestikon.

Without the large numbers of armed men that only ELAS could provide, the British Special Forces were limited to small-scale harassing operations. On 19 September, Pat signalled Cairo that the *Andartes* were fighting little, if at all, and deceiving the British as to their strength, locations and ammunition. Two days later, he told Prentice that attacks on defended positions needed an assault force, which he had not got. The RSR was a support force, the *Closandartes* would not press home an attack and Yannoulis's troops ran away. When, on 27 September, a well-guarded German column of 1,500 men came through Vatochori towards Florina, Lieutenant Robinson's section of the RSR could do nothing; the commando was too small to engage the enemy directly unless everything was right for an ambush. The next night, Lieutenant Chalkley and another section of the RSR, together with Kite and the commando, went to ambush a column of 1,000 foot soldiers, 60 vehicles and 36 artillery pieces. This time, a low mist prevented them from taking positions with a good escape route and the ambush was aborted. The Germans shelled the commandos' position and the station at Boufi, wrecking a house and killing two people.

A combined operation with the Long Range Desert Group finally managed a successful ambush on the road between Vigla and Florina. Just before dawn of 21 October, Stormonth-Darling blew a culvert behind a German column, while Tozer and Kite blew the road in front. Most of the *Closandartes* ran away, but the commando stayed and shot up the trapped column. The Germans countered with tank, mortar and machine-gun fire, but the attackers suffered no casualties. Two trucks were destroyed by the explosion, eighteen damaged, and eighty Germans were wounded; several cartloads of dead were later removed from Florina. Just after dawn, Spitfires from the 'Balkan Air Force' (composed of units of the RAF and South African Air Force, operating out of Bari) arrived to give air support and set three more trucks alight.

It soon became obvious that the retreating Germans were not going to protect their flanks by making drives into the surrounding mountains: Pat was able to re-establish a stable base at Vapsori. As station commander, linguist and intelligence specialist, he was practically fixed in the village. Pat only left the station for a few days in October to visit his most distant operational group and, briefly, to move his headquarters to another village about ninety minutes away when the Germans came too close for comfort.

As the Germans withdrew north towards Yugoslavia, Pat monitored the signals and kept up a flow of reports on enemy garrisons, rail traffic through Florina and the movement of enemy columns along the roads through the Monastir Gap to Yugoslavia. He sent a stream of information and supplies to the three RSR sections, the *Closandartes* and the commando. Explosives, clothing and ammunition were dropped at Argos Orestikon and then brought 40 kilometres by mule to locked stores in Vapsori for distribution. Most of the Special Forces were carrying out operation after operation; the rest were working frantically to keep up a supply of food, ammunition, warm clothes and explosives. The supply problem was complicated by the distances and terrain, bad weather, the scarcity of mules and the reluctance of runners and *Andartes* to cross the roads used by the enemy. Pat's notebooks for the autumn of 1944 are full of the briefest practical notes and scraps of information about enemy movements, targets and logistics. He had no time for reflection or descriptive diary entries. Intelligence was flooding in: a huge amount of information, much of it inaccurate, had to be sifted and correlated. There were reports to write for area command in Pendalofos and headquarters in Cairo, signals to send and receive, and deserters to interrogate. Medical care had to be provided for the wounded and the base had to be kept clean: vermin, sickness and infectious disease were serious dangers to SOE missions in the mountains. On 30 October, Captain Chapman, RAMC was summoned urgently to Vapsori to treat two wounded Poles attached to the commando. He found that the base was well-kept and sanitary.[4]

Pat also had to deal with ELAS. When it came to combat, the *Andartes* were keen, Pat wrote, but lacked discipline. In the Klidhi pass they had run, without firing a shot, from 100 German foot soldiers without tanks, artillery or mortars. Yannoulis was now the *kapetanios* of 1st Battalion, 28th Regiment and continued to give support in word but not deed.[5] Pat had recently received 1,000 sovereigns, nearly 8 kilos of twenty-two carat gold; he was waiting for Yannoulis's bill for August and had promised financial support for 550 men for September. It was galling to have to go on paying ELAS so much when they delivered so little. ELAS had even tried, unsuccessfully, to restrict the mission's movements on the pretence of danger from armed villages. In contrast, Arrianos, who was no longer in Pat's area, continued to prove his willingness to take on the Germans, even at the cost of heavy losses. Pat's diary records an attack by Arrianos' battalion on the town of Kozani at the end of September, in which he had taken two enemy guard posts for the loss of eleven dead and twenty-four wounded *Andartes*.

Cairo issued a series of contradictory directives about the surrender of enemy forces. The first, on 6 September, forbade liaison officers to accept the surrender of any German group smaller than a division (10,000 to 15,000 men) and went on in the same vein of wishful thinking: 'Surrender of all Hun forces in Greece ideal and for them to remain *in situ* with arms and equipment feeding themselves and await arrival of Allied Forces.' Liaison officers must report efforts to surrender and not accept any surrender less than complete, make no promise, guarantee or comment, and refer to higher authority (Cairo) for instructions. They should attempt to stop small parties surrendering themselves, and prevent the *Andartes* from getting hold of their weapons. Any Poles, French, Russians or Czechs must be treated as Huns. NOAH'S ARK was the first task and the RSR should not be wasted guarding enemy equipment or prisoners.

Two weeks later, on 21 September, a new order cancelled the first. British officers should not encourage small individual enemy detachments to surrender but should not stop them offering. The Germans should be persuaded to surrender to the British rather than to the *Andartes* and every approach for surrender reported to Cairo. Pat signalled back a report from his spies: 'Huns in Florina say to local people we will surrender to Russians or British but not to *Andartes*.' Three days later, Rennos spent five hours talking to the German guard post at Mikri Vigla in the presence of an RSR officer, Lieutenant Chalkley, and Peter Kite. The Germans were willing to surrender to the British but not to ELAS, but Chalkley was not allowed to accept. When he finally left, one of the Germans was in tears, saying 'goot English'.

A third directive arrived on 30 September:

Hun surrender. 1. Make Hun aware your presence sole channel negotiations, as prior instructions. 2. Only discuss surrender with Senior Officer in command. When Hun approach made, report fully when unit prepared to surrender. Cairo will instruct. Method to be settled between Hun envoy and ALO [Allied Liaison Officer] after instructions from Cairo. Make sure understood terms now not unconditional and may be altered.

Pat signalled that it would be impossible to take surrenders of small detachments if every case had to be referred to Cairo for instructions. During the delay, guard posts might be strengthened or replaced. Most guard posts would give in, but many contained one or two soldiers who would give the game away if they got the chance. Either Cairo should give officers on the ground a blank cheque, or tell them to leave small detachments entirely alone and concentrate on getting the formal surrender of all troops in the area.

On 8 October, orders changed again: all negotiations for surrender of the German army in North Greece should be made in conjunction with local commanders of ELAS Ninth Division and with ELAS GHQ. General Sarafis had been authorized to accept the surrender of Germans in all ELAS areas. Negotiations for major surrender must be referred phase by phase to Cairo for information and decision. This was an absurdity, which ignored the realities of geography and communication. Ninth Division and ELAS GHQ were far away from the action, and British officers on the ground might easily be a day's march away from radio communications. Pat wrote: 'the German soldier generally, with the exception of the SS, was ready to give in, provided he was sure he was surrendering to the British and not to the *Andartes*. I could have obtained numbers of desertions during NOAH'S ARK had I been allowed to do so.'[6]

ELAS itself was distracted by the outbreak of a conflict between Macedonians and Greeks. On 11 October, Pat wrote to warn Prentice of serious trouble in 2nd Battalion, 28th Regiment (2/28), which had been raised by a Macedonian known as Gotchi (or Gotse). Gotchi came from the village of Melas and his men were also Macedonians from the Vitsi villages. Yannoulis suspected that Gotchi had been 'infected' with Macedonian separatism by Peyo. Without a word to Pat, Yannoulis had ordered 2/28 away from Vitsi to Mount Vermion. Gotchi refused to go: his men were Macedonians and their place was there in Macedonia. They looked on Greek-speaking Vermion as a foreign country whereas Bitola, over the border in Yugoslavia, was almost like home. Gotchi and his battalion commander had a furious row, leading to drawn pistols. Gotchi was restrained and placed under arrest. As a result, 2/28 was in open revolt and refusing to obey ELAS orders. About forty *Andartes* had been seen near Gavros, going north 'to get arms from Tito'. They were thought to be going to Deyan, the partisan leader in Prespa. Disaffection had spread to some of the men in the second company of 1/28, although its *kapetanios*, Keravnos, remained loyal and pro-Greek; his company had been giving willing support to the British. ELAS planned to disarm the rebels, then rearm the reliable men and place them with others to maintain the battalion's strength. Pat went to ELAS regimental headquarters in Flambouro the next day to see Yannoulis and try to make sure that he kept his troops in position on the road between Albania and Florina.[7]

Gotchi went to Agios Germanos, taking his whole battalion and a good many villagers with him. Then, once the Germans were out of the way, he moved his men north to Bitola in Yugoslavia where he had excellent relations with the partisans. Here the Communist Party held sway and the Macedonian flag, a gold star on a red ground, flew all over town.[8] On 17 October, Pat warned Cairo that the Macedonian problem would be a running sore after the war unless the Greek National Government had a firm, consistent, liberal policy for the Slav-speaking community.

Finally, the German withdrawal was over. On 1 November 1944, the British entered Florina: Captain Tozer, Peter Kite and Gerry Livieratos were the first in, followed the day after by Pat with the radio set.[9] However, it was not the happy arrival they expected. Although most of the population had been anxiously waiting for them, there was hardly a welcome for the mission, Pompforce (the British army liberation force) or the troops of the Fourth Indian Regiment. ELAS and EAM had issued a word-of-mouth directive that any fraternization would be severely punished: a large number of pro-British were arrested by ELAS and accused of having collaborated with the Germans. Rennos himself threatened Livieratos with punishment by the People's Court as a traitor for co-operating with the British and serving with the AMM as an interpreter.[10]

The Communist Party controlled movement by issuing passes for travel between Florina and Bitola, and was trying to levy 1,500 sovereigns from the townspeople. Tension between Greeks and Slavs was running high: most of the villagers were Slav and proud to call themselves 'Macedonians, not Greeks'. The Greek populace would normally rise as one man to meet a Slav threat but was disunited because only ELAS offered leadership and ELAS was now only popular with the communists. ELAS itself was frightened by Gotchi. On the other side of the coin, the Slav population distrusted ELAS in particular and the Greeks in general. They had been fooled by Axis and Bulgarian promises of an independent Macedonia; now they were wary of coming out too soon in favour of either Gotchi or Tempo's Macedonians.

A British presence was highly desirable, Pat recommended, as a way of diminishing the communist hold on the population; Indian troops, though, would offend all sections of the population. Fine troops though they were, the Greeks would think of them merely as 'black men' and take their presence as an insult. The sooner a Greek government sent representatives and set up a civil administration the better. In the meantime, there was a great deal of military administration to do, supplies to organize, accounts to reconcile and reports to write. Kite signed off the report to Prentice on actions in NOAH'S ARK,[11] to which Pat added a summary:

> *Salient features of NOAH'S ARK operations in this area, reported by Captain Evans.*
>
> Good work by Poles and Czechs (henceforth 'Commando')
>
> Ditto by all langs [language operatives], all of whom have proved themselves to be more than interpreters and have taken part in almost every operation.
>
> Considerable hardship due to bad weather, which in addition hampered operations, the RSR role being shooting, not demolitions. In the low cloud, which sometimes continued for days at a time, the visibility was not more than twenty yards.
>
> A genuine effort on the part of the *Andarte* units to achieve some sort of a result, an effort which was, however, largely nullified by the shocking inefficiency of most *Andartes* and their commanders, and also by the rebellion of Gotsi, which in the area north and west of Florina caused ELAS to lose all interest in the Germans.
>
> The '*Closandartes*' cannot be described as anything but a failure.
>
> Consistently outstanding work by Sgt Kite.
>
> Signed by P.H. Evans, Florina, 15 Nov 44.

Pat was exhausted, fed up with ELAS, EAM and the Macedonian imbroglio, and was itching to get away. On 27 November 1944 he handed over Fertiliser to Captain Tozer and left. His departure did not go unobserved: the Communist Party Secretary in Florina reported to KKE's Macedonia headquarters that Evans had gone to Athens.[12]

Chapter Six

Separatism and Civil War: the Macedonian Question

Pat left for Athens on 23 November. The road headed east from Florina across the plain before it divided, one branch running north through the Monastir Gap to Yugoslavia, the other turning southwards through the Klidhi Pass, skirting the marshes to Kozani. In 1944 this was one of the very few metalled roads in Western Macedonia and not much better than a cart track. In Kozani, Pat found his comrades from Boodle, who were due to leave Greece via Salonika. He stopped for long enough to take two group photographs and have them developed by a local photographer before continuing his journey. Modern travellers have a choice of motorway routes that will take them from Kozani to Athens within the day. Alternatively, they can follow the little roads south, through the plains of Thessaly and the heartland of Roumeli, to reach the capital after a night's stop. In 1944, the roads were in an atrocious state after the fighting in pursuit of the retreating Germans and it was a long, winding, jolting drive before Pat reached Athens on the 26th.

Athens had suffered terribly since Pat was last there in 1937. Occupation had brought looting and large-scale expropriation of food and natural resources. Harvests fell catastrophically and farmers were reluctant to sell their depleted stocks. Food distribution faltered and failed. The winter of 1941–42 brought first hunger, then famine and starvation; malnutrition encouraged tuberculosis, influenza and infectious diseases; the birth rate plummeted and the death rate soared. Tens of thousands of people died of starvation in Athens before relief began. Nobody knows the exact numbers but the Red Cross estimated that a quarter of a million people died in Greece between 1941 and 1943 from starvation or illness resulting from the famine.[1]

The occupation had wrecked the structures of civilian administration and played havoc with social norms. Under the occupying powers, cheating the regime became a patriotic duty; survival often depended on the black market and the boundary between resistance and brigandage was blurred. The gendarmerie's role in law enforcement was ambiguous to say the least. So too was the position of the security battalions, set up by the collaborationist Prime Minister Ioannis Rallis in 1943 as a nationalist defence force and counter to the left-wing EAM/ELAS resistance.

In the shadows, to the right, lurked the underground royalist militia 'X' ('Chi') formed by Colonel Grivas to oppose first the Germans and then the communists. EAM itself had eaten away at the state by co-opting local civil servants and setting up its own shadow administration. By the summer of 1944, civic order had almost broken down in Athens, with sporadic but ferocious street-fighting between small groups of ELAS *Andartes* on the one side and the gendarmerie, security battalions and 'X' on the other, accompanied by round-ups, public hangings and summary executions.

EAM/ELAS had created a Political Committee for National Liberation (PEEA) up in the mountains as the basis for a future government, while the 'legitimist' government waited in Cairo. King George II of the Hellenes stayed in London, hoping the situation would soon allow his return to Greece as a constitutional monarch. To complicate matters further, while the king had earned Churchill's gratitude and support by his stand against the Germans, the government-in-exile was solidly republican. Georgios Papandreou, who had taken the leadership in April 1944, was an anti-monarchist social democrat. His 'national unity' cabinet included ministers nominated by PEEA and approved by the communists.

Papandreou came back to Greece as prime minister on 18 October 1944, accompanied by his cabinet, Ambassador Leeper and General Sir Robert Scobie. They found a country on the edge of starvation, with runaway inflation, no proper law enforcement and a desperate need for reconciliation between the armed factions of left and right. Return to normality depended on disarming and disbanding the resistance groups and reconstructing the army, police and gendarmerie; the alternative would be revolution and civil war.

General Scobie met General Sarafis, the military commander of ELAS, and Napoleon Zervas, leader of the right-wing guerrillas EDES, in Athens on 22 November to discuss demobilization. Although EDES was willing, the much larger ELAS was reluctant to relinquish the power of the gun; Sarafis would only accept an order signed by the whole cabinet, including its PEEA members. The cabinet rejected a decree drafted by Papandreou but on 28 November approved one drafted by PEEA. PEEA then refused to sign its own text and presented a third version, which demanded the demobilization of returning Greek regular forces and the retention of ELAS weapons. Papandreou refused.

There was also a shadow from the north hanging over the power struggle in Athens. Although EAM/ELAS and the Communist Party seemed to be in control of the mountains, Gotchi's revolt in October had signalled a resurgence of the Slav-Macedonian independence movement; an irruption of separatist violence from Yugoslavia, backed by the Yugoslav Macedonian partisans, would throw the Balkans into chaos.

Pat set himself to warn the British authorities. Four days after arriving in Athens, on 1 December 1944, his 31st birthday, he completed a 'REPORT ON THE FREE MACEDONIA MOVEMENT IN AREA FLORINA 1944.'[2] This was not a dry intelligence assessment but an impassioned effort to convey the urgency and complexity of the 'Macedonian question'. Pat set the scene by describing the linguistic and cultural make-up of this remote region, about which he cared deeply:

> The one salient fact about the area in question is very rarely grasped. Englishmen, even those who know Greece, fail to grasp it because few of them ever go so far north. Greeks fail to grasp it for two reasons. First, they do not want to. It is to their advantage to believe that all places which are marked 'Greece' on the map are, or ought to be, Greek in sympathy and in every other way; Greek by nature as it were; they do not wish to realize that many of the inhabitants of Macedonia-in-Greece have almost as good reasons for considering themselves Macedonians as they themselves have for considering themselves Greek. It is a slight case of wishful thinking, a sort of hoodwinking which is an inseparable part of the Great Idea. The second reason is that, or so at least I am told, successive Greek Governments since the liberation of Slavophone Greece from the Turks have been, despite their various political complexions, alike in one thing, that they have carefully fostered this delusion, as if to give the impression both to their own people and to the world that there was no Slav minority in Greece at all; whereas, if a foreigner who did not know Greece were to visit the Florina region and from that to form his idea of the country as a whole, he could conclude that it was the Greeks who were the minority. It is predominantly a Slav region, not a Greek one. The language of the home, and usually also of the fields, the village street, the market, is Macedonian, a Slav language... Even those who know Greek prefer to speak Macedonian when they can. A stranger who says 'Good Morning' in Greek will get the same reply, but if he says it in Macedonian he will get a flood of welcoming phrases in addition.
>
> Greek is regarded as almost a foreign language and the Greeks are distrusted as something alien, even if not, in the full sense of the word, as foreigners. This obvious fact, almost too obvious to be stated, that the region is Slav by nature and not Greek cannot be overemphasized! It is after all the start of the whole problem, and it is only by bearing it in mind that a satisfactory solution may be reached, instead of some botched-up remedy which will invite trouble later.

It is also important to emphasize that the inhabitants, just as they are not Greeks, are also not Bulgarians or Serbs or Croats. They are Macedonians.

Although there was a degree of loyalty to the Greek state, most Macedonians were actuated by a feeling for Macedonia and, most powerfully, a local patriotism in the form of an attachment to their own bit of country, their *patridha*. Gotsi refused the order to move from Mount Vitsi to Mount Vermion on the grounds that he and his men were Macedonians, fighting for Macedonia, and that was where they should be: Vermion might be in Western Macedonia, but Vitsi was Gotsi's *patridha*. It had often been said, before the war, that Macedonians were more susceptible to communism than the Greeks, but Pat thought that the ordinary Macedonian villager was more interested in prosperity than in politics; what he wanted above all was to be left in peace:

He is curiously neutral; he adopts a protective colouring and, like the chameleon, can change it when necessary…. An old man at Korifi put this aspect of the Macedonian character very clearly to me. He was a Slav, yet had been *proedros* of his own village, Vapsori, during Metaxas's regime. In consequence he was now out of favour with EAM and ELAS. He told me: 'You see, we have had so many different masters that now, whoever comes along, we say (placing his hands together and smiling pleasantly and making a little bow) *Kalos orisate*! [Welcome.]' It was most eloquent. It is this perfect duplicity of the Macedonians which makes them difficult to know. It is hard to find out what they are thinking. A third man present at the conversation completed the thing by saying: 'At bottom, our attitude is really this. We don't mind if the state takes away part of our produce as tax; five, ten, even fifteen per cent. But let the state be reasonable; let it only take a moderate amount, so that I know that what I work for, what I sweat for, will at the end be mine. If I go out on the hill this evening and spend the night making charcoal, what do I get? Only a few drachmas, about enough for a packet of cigarettes. You see, our mountains are poor, and we have so very little. What we really want is for some rich country like England or America to open up Macedonia, exploit her for her tobacco and her untouched minerals. Then everyone would draw his pay every week and there would be plenty to eat and good clothes to wear. Greece can't do it; she is too poor.'

The same man, who had fought as a machine-gunner in the Albanian war, eventually joined Gotchi's rebellion and defected to Yugoslavia in the name of an independent Macedonia.

Years of suppression had made Greek Macedonians apathetic: they would follow the dominant power and look to whoever seemed likely to treat them better. A nationality of their own was less important than the freedom to speak their own language, to live unmolested and improve their standard of living. Despite the pro-Bulgarian propaganda pumped out by the Axis offices in Florina and Kastoria during the occupation and the Axis support for the *Komitadjis*

> MACEDONIANS as a whole do not seem to be really attracted to BULGARIA, and some were actually afraid that she would have treated them as an inferior minority, as the Serbs and Greeks already do. If the area I am acquainted with had been genuinely pro-Bulgar, all the villages in it would probably be armed, whereas the only ones that did take arms were those situated on the low ground on the fringes of the Vitsi mountain pass. The mountain area proper was always free of armed villagers, though not of informers who would betray *Andartes* and British personnel to the Germans. Those of the inhabitants who were not pro-Greek – that is to say, the majority – were either uneasily neutral or else filled with a rather vague aspiration towards a free Macedonia run on Left Wing lines.

Although Greeks and Macedonians seemed to live together amicably in Florina, bad feeling between the two communities ran deep. Both sides had committed atrocities during the Resistance; psychological warfare and propaganda had further embittered the situation. If this erupted into violence, it would be vicious: 'Mountains produce men who are tough and hardy and who, when they fight, if their passions are engaged, fight with fury, and underneath the skin of almost every peasant, whatever his good qualities, lies somewhere concealed a murderous materialist.'

The weakness of the fledgling government had allowed Macedonian nationalist feeling to rise and the danger to grow. Even among educated Greeks, the attitude towards the Slavs was 'usually stupid, uninformed and brutal to a degree that makes one despair of any understanding ever being created between the two people.' Many Greeks either did not know that there was a Slav-speaking minority in the country or condemned them as Bulgars who ought to be either killed or sent back to Bulgaria.

Gotchi was said to be in Monastir, in Yugoslavia. He had 500 armed men at the time of his revolt and was said to have collected a further 500 to 1,000 unarmed civilians, some taken by force, others going of their own free will. He had been joined by Peyo of Gavros, who had taken arms from the Germans to fight the *Andartes* in pursuit of an independent Macedonia; another petty guerrilla leader had also taken his band to join Gotchi's revolt. Pat felt that these were minor figures, whose movement was just a villagers' revolt. By contrast, the Yugoslav partisan leaders Abbas, Tempo (Tito's representative) and Deyan posed a real threat: they were better-educated, better-trained, more determined and much more effective fighters. Abbas had told a British officer that he was not a communist but a nationalist: all he wanted was 'Macedonia for the Macedonians'. Deyan had been busy recruiting partisans and making propaganda for Macedonia during the spring and summer of 1944. By July, Tito and Tempo controlled three brigades of Macedonian partisans, totalling about 1,200 men in all. Tempo advocated a plebiscite. If he insisted and was refused, he would probably resort to an armed rising. On the other hand, a fair plebiscite was likely to result in demands for a free Macedonia, which would lead to disaster:

> There can be no independent Macedonia. Even if one regards it, as I do, as right, in the abstract, that there should be, one has to concede that practically it is undesirable.
>
> A Macedonian rising would be resisted most violently by the Greeks, who would probably rise in a body from all over Greece to beat it down. In particular the demand for Salonika would rouse the Greeks to fury. The result would be an extremely bloody war out of which no good would come.
>
> The frontiers of Greece, at any rate between say Prespa and Kaimatsalan, must remain unaltered.
>
> At the same time Greece, if she is not to be severely troubled by her Macedonian minority, and also in the interests of equity, must treat that minority well; firmly, yes, but with friendship, without discrimination. I am not sanguine of this happening. But it is not impossible.

Pat delivered his report to the embassy just as the crisis in Athens was coming to a head. On Friday, 1 December 1944 the ELAS police group refused to hand over its duties to the National Guard. Prime Minister Papandreou called a cabinet meeting without notifying the PEEA-nominated ministers; that night, six of the seven resigned, followed the next day by the seventh. What remained of the cabinet approved a decree dissolving both ELAS and EDES. The Communist Party announced a demonstration for Sunday, 3 December to be followed by a general strike.

On Sunday, a crowd of demonstrators closed with the police in Constitution Square and shots were fired from the police into the crowd. Some said that the crowd fired first, others that the police fired without provocation and with no response. Eye-witnesses, officials and supporters of factions on the left and right gave widely differing accounts at the time, as have historians ever since. It was very hard to be sure: random shots were not uncommon in Athens. The one certainty was that people now lay dead and wounded, although there was no agreement about their numbers. After the shooting was over, British troops cleared the square without using force. ELAS occupied a number of police stations and armed columns were reported to be marching on the capital.

The next morning, *The Times* unequivocally laid the blame on the police. Under a headline 'Crowd fired on in Athens: repeated volleys by police' the article began: 'Seeds of civil war were well and truly sown by Athens police this morning when they fired on a demonstration of children and youths.' According to a special correspondent, police had opened fire with rifles and tommy guns on a procession of mostly girls and boys. 'The crowd immediately fell flat to escape the bullets, but the police continued firing. When they stopped the demonstrators got to their feet and started to pick up the wounded and dead and the police then fired on them again.' This, wrote the correspondent, was a signal for wild and savage firing to break out from police headquarters and government ministries, which 'continued sporadically for nearly an hour in spite of violent protests by individual British officers.' The passive presence of British units served only to associate Britain with a 'Fascist action'.

Papandreou tendered his resignation but the king (who was still in London) refused to accept it; Churchill wanted Papandreou to continue and there was no obvious replacement. There was, though, a clear possibility that ELAS was about to take control of Athens and, indeed, Greece as a whole.

A series of telegrams from Churchill to General Scobie and Rex Leeper, sent in the early hours of 5 December, made no bones about the dangers of the situation and authorized them to take whatever military and political action might be necessary, however drastic. In a telegram to Leeper, marked 'Personal and top secret' and sent at 3.20 am, Churchill wrote:

1. This is no time to dabble in Greek politics or to imagine that Greek politicians of varying shades can affect the situation. You should not worry about the Greek government compositions. The matter is one of life and death.

2. You must force Papandreou to stand to his duty and assure him he will be supported by all our forces if he does so. Should he resign, he should be locked up till he comes to his senses, when the fighting will probably be over. It might be well that he should be in bed and inaccessible. The day has long gone past when any particular group of Greek politicians can influence this mob rising. His only chance is to come through with us.[3]

Churchill ordered Leeper to support Scobie in every possible way and, indeed, to encourage him into vigorous and decisive action; a quarter of an hour later Churchill forwarded Leeper a copy of his instructions to Scobie so that there should be no room for doubt:

2. You are responsible for maintaining order in Athens and for neutralizing or destroying all EAM-ELAS bands approaching the city. You may make any regulations you like for the strict control of the streets or for the rounding up of any number of truculent persons. Naturally ELAS will try to put women and children in the van where shooting may occur. You must be clever about this and avoid mistakes. But do not hesitate to fire at any armed male in Athens who assails the British authority or Greek authority with which we are working. It would be well of course if your command were reinforced by the authority of some Greek Government, and Papandreou is being told by Leeper to stop and help. Do not, however, hesitate to act as if you were in a conquered city where a rebellion was in progress.
3. With regard to ELAS bands approaching from the outside, you should surely be able with your armour to give some of these a lesson, which will make others unlikely to try. You may count on my support in all reasonable and sensible action taken on this basis. We have to hold and dominate Athens. It would be a great thing for you to succeed in this without bloodshed if possible but also with bloodshed if necessary.[4]

British regular commanders had been deeply suspicious of SOE's negative view of EAM/ELAS and KKE; when fighting broke out, Prentice was sent back from Athens to Salonika, which became the designated base for remaining elements of Force 133 pending evacuation from Greece.[5] Pat, though, was not among them. Although his military mission in Greece had ended with his hand-over in Florina and he was not part of any unit fighting in Athens, his report had been noticed. A trained intelligence officer with fluent Greek and first-hand knowledge of local politics was too valuable an asset to waste. Pat was pressed into service as a go-between, unhappily shuttling back and forth between the British Embassy, Papandreou and the Greek cabinet.

In London, Labour MP Seymour Cocks tabled an amendment to the response to the king's speech to the House of Commons, regretting that it

contains no assurance that His Majesty's forces will not be used to disarm the friends of democracy in Greece and other parts of Europe, or suppress those popular movements which have valorously assisted in the defeat of the enemy and upon whose success we must rely the future friendly co-operation in Europe.

This was political dynamite, tantamount to a motion of censure. It had to be debated and put to a vote. If the government lost the vote, it would fall.

The debate was set for 8 December. On the day before, *The Times* published a graphic account of events in Athens, which was less sympathetic to ELAS now that British troops were coming under fire:

> War has been going on in Athens since last night, a horrible, difficult kind of war, in which British and Greeks have been killed. Fortunately the casualties are in no way commensurate with the ammunition expended for the city has been filled with the sound of gunfire since dawn, and so far as can be ascertained the dead on both sides do not exceed a dozen. It is horrible warfare because it is being in the main fought between British troops and their Greek friends, and is as repugnant to the one as to the other; it is difficult because it is street fighting, with most of the casualties caused by sniping from roof-tops.

The RAF had been in action too, strafing ELAS positions, and there were some reports of ELAS surrenders, which *The Times* took as a sign that ELAS was not supported by the mass of the people. The main problem faced by the British troops was 'a small number of armed ELAS men concealed in private houses, where they fire with rifles and sometimes machine-guns on everybody approaching.'

On 9 December *The Times* carried a word-for-word account of the previous day's debate in Parliament. Seymour Cocks had moved the amendment in emotional terms: 'To-day, on the sacred soil of Athens, in the shadow of the Acropolis, British soldiers and Greek patriots lay dead side by side, each with an allied bullet in his heart.' He asked the government immediately 'to put an end to this fratricidal strife' and accused them of far greater sympathy with what he called 'the Greek dictatorship exiled in Egypt' than with 'the popular resistance movement fighting in the mountains of Greece'.

> I find it difficult to suppress my grief, horror, and indignation at these mad and mischievous proceedings, but as calmly as I can I would ask the Prime Minister and the Government to re-consider their action, to reverse their policy, and retrace their footsteps before it is too late. The present dictatorship in Greece should be replaced, as quickly as possible, by a coalition Government of all parties.

Churchill was thoroughly prepared and in robust form. He stressed the need for a democracy founded on free elections and universal suffrage:

> Democracy, I say, is not based on violence or terrorism, but on reason, on fair play, on freedom, on respecting other people's rights as well as their ambitions. Democracy is no harlot, to be picked up in the street by a man with a tommy gun. I trust the people, the mass of the people, in almost any country, but I like to make sure that it is the people, and not a gang of bandits from the mountains or from the countryside, who think that by violence they can overturn constituted authority, in some cases ancient Parliaments, Governments, and States.

Churchill spelled out the steps Britain had taken to avoid the danger of a communist-inspired takeover after the Germans left, the provision of aid to Greece and the creation of a legitimate cross-party government, up to the moment when

> the carefully prepared forces of ELAS began to infiltrate into Athens and into the Piraeus. The other bodies began to move down from the northern hills towards the city. The six EAM Ministers resigned from the Government at this moment. One gentleman, I believe, was a little slow, but on being rung up on the telephone and told he would be killed if he did not come out he made haste to follow the general practice. The intention of the 'friends of democracy' who now entered the city was to overthrow by violence the constitutional Government of Greece and to install themselves without anything in the nature of an election as the expression of the people's will.

Even before the Foreign Secretary, Anthony Eden, wound up the debate, spelling out the government's case in detail, the leader of the official Labour opposition, Arthur Greenwood, threw in the towel and 'proposed to ask his friends not to vote for the amendment'. The British government should, he added optimistically, 'get all the sections of Greek opinion together with a view to an understanding on the question of the disarming of all armed bands.'

There had been talk in the British press of a peace offer by ELAS, but Churchill was sceptical and on 9 December ordered Scobie to stand firm, cabling: 'The clear objective is to defeat EAM. The ending of the fighting is subsidiary to this. I am ordering large reinforcements to come to Athens and Field Marshal Alexander will probably be with you in a few days.'[6] Churchill's scepticism was justified and the situation in Athens continued to deteriorate. On 11 December *The Times* reported that the RAF had bombed strong ELAS formations approaching the city, and

British headquarters came under mortar fire. British efforts to clear the city by day were largely undone by ELAS infiltration at night. The next day, ELAS was reported to have as many as 25,000 men massed in or around the capital, while British reinforcements were heading towards the city. Field Marshal Alexander (who had taken over as Supreme Commander Mediterranean) and Harold Macmillan, the Minister Resident in the Mediterranean, made a flying visit to assess the situation. Scobie's headquarters issued a report that ELAS snipers were picketing all routes out of the city and shelling by 75mm cannon had become heavier. Serious clashes took place between ELAS and British troops; ELAS broke into a barracks but were driven out after tanks were called. *The Times* reported that ELAS controlled four-fifths of Athens, but British reinforcements had arrived and were in action. Strafing by Spitfires had ended the shelling and rifle-fire was no longer heard in the city centre, but the water supply to the British sector had been cut off and food was very scarce. Wild rumours went the rounds. EAM claimed that 10,000 people had been killed by RAF bombing and strafing in a suburb of Athens and that massive ELAS forces would overrun the British. On 14 December, Seymour Cocks caused an uproar in the House of Commons by asking 'how long the Government intended to go on with the policy of murder in Greece?' In Athens, both sides were exploring ways of sidestepping the issue of the monarchy and forming an interim government with the Archbishop of Athens, Damaskinos, as regent: on 15 December, a message went from Papandreou to the King of Greece, via Macmillan and Leeper, advising the immediate establishment of a three-man Council of Regency with the archbishop as president. Pat left the same day, flying first to Bari in Italy and then on to Cairo. He was tired, but boiling with thoughts about events in Greece.

On 23 December Pat wrote to Jill, for the first time in months:

Tonight's series of letters will be very disconnected. I'm just sitting here in a lovely old houseboat with the line 'that's my serpent of old Nile' running through my head as it has done ever since I began my re-acquaintance with this City 48 hours ago. …I expect from my telegram, and by putting 2 and 2 together, you will now have gathered where I was roughly from September last year till about the middle of this month. Don't worry, even in retrospect! It wasn't terribly adventurous, though it was enormously interesting (and rather harassing and, in the long run, tiring). In my work, both in peace and in war, I seem so far to have been fated to do things which don't turn out as they should, and which don't end in any great adventure or personal success for me, but which do certainly increase my experience and knowledge of life – I have had my nose well rubbed in it one way and another. I suppose it's all a preparation for post-war, in which I think we shall simply settle down and live happily ever after. I'm not yet allowed to tell you all about my doings, but I believe I shall be soon. Till then I will keep mum. It would be a pity, having been so security minded and well behaved all along, to go and spoil it at the end.

I had some contact (official) with the Greek cabinet while I was in Athens. Mostly they are a set of pathetic professional politicians – a slightly greasy pack of cards. But Papandreou is a good man, I think. A fairly firm character, reasonable, and appears to be a genuine democrat.

Please do NOT take on trust anything said by the Left in England. They are a disgrace and make me foam with rage. If they knew what thugs they were sympathizing with (EAM/ELAS) they would change their tune a bit, these well-meaning Labourites. I have no inclination to unfold the whole thing in letters: I have had a bellyful of it and want to forget it for a while. But one thing you can be sure of: if all we are fighting for is to survive in Greece – democracy, freedom and rule by reasonableness as against horrible barbarity and secret police methods – ELAS must be broken.

The British left wing, and even some responsible newspapers, are disgracing themselves terribly by yapping piously and with conviction about a situation and country of which they know nothing. I could go through all of their statements I have so far seen and blue-pencil one by one their blunders in sheer matters of fact: blunders which form essential links in their arguments. How can they hope to be right, knowing so little? Greece is perhaps the most difficult of countries to know about – always paradoxical, and extremely hard for an Englishman to understand. In addition, the present situation is a complex one. I have been learning it first hand for a longish time past – and not from the Hôtel Grande Bretagne, which is made of marble and stands in the centre of Athens and is where the correspondents observe the situation from – and even so I have to admit I don't know it really well. But you can feel confident we are not backing the equivalent of Franco or Denikin [the Russian Tsarist general who led the 'White Terror']... We are trying to dissolve the threat of a tyranny which, if it was hanging over the British people instead of the Greeks, would fill everyone with horror – including Arthur Greenwood and that absurd little sentimental exhibitionist Seymour Cocks. Greenwood suggests negotiating with the EAM leaders. Has he ever *tried* negotiating with that type, a type so crooked as to be unknown in British politics, and learnt that it is utterly futile, I wonder? Obviously not. I have. I know. Everything I say in the Greek business comes out of an experience more thorough and complete than I am allowed to tell you yet.

I was very relieved to get away from Athens. I like the Greeks a good deal, in fact am a confirmed Philhellene, and sympathize with all parties except the extreme Right (near Fascists) and the extreme Left (thugs of an almost unbelievable crookedness and brutality). Among the people they killed, a murder not a battle casualty, was a very good friend of mine. So I sat around, or trotted hither and yon on odd jobs – going to the Embassy, the Greek Cabinet and Papandreou, the Greek Foreign Secretary and so on – and felt miserable; just emotionally torturing myself. I shan't be easy in my mind till the matter is settled.

On New Year's Eve, he wrote again about the events in Athens:

I had no personal troubles but the military and political troubles, Greeks killing Englishmen and vice versa, churned me up a great deal. I am – you must be prepared for this when I come home! – more pro-British than ever (though critical, often enough); very attached to our own people; at the same time, and in spite of a good deal of disillusionment and disappointment, I do like Greece and the Greeks, and am a confirmed, though again critical, Philhellene. So the whole business got me down. And the attitude of the supposedly enlightened part of the British press & Parliament, supporting what my friend John Mulgan calls 'the Fascism of the left', was maddening. And a corporal who had once been through adventures and times both black and gay with me, got shot through the head. Altogether, it got me down, and I just hadn't the spirit to put pen to paper. Anyway, all the things I had on my mind I wasn't allowed to say, except that I love you, and that wasn't news.

Added to which, the rebels got my kit, including all my silk pyjamas and shirts, and a bit of silk I was keeping for you, and all my papers, which were to have been raw material for a book about my last 15 months!

Rebellion and the start of civil war in Athens dominated the news from Greece, but behind the scenes the War Cabinet was worrying about the strategic and political future of the wider Balkan region, stretching beyond Greece to Yugoslavia, Bulgaria and Albania. In the short term, there was a risk of another Balkan war, with a confrontation between British forces on the one hand and Macedonian partisans on the other, possibly with Yugoslav backing, which could also bring the Americans and Russians into the conflict. Both Yugoslavia and Bulgaria appeared to be reasserting their claims over Greek Macedonia and there was talk of a union between Yugoslavia and Bulgaria, which would upset the balance of power. As the briefing memorandum for the 11 December War Cabinet meeting put it:

> No sooner was the ink dry on the Bulgarian Armistice than signs began to appear which showed that Tito's Yugoslavs were beginning to think about Yugoslav-Bulgarian federation, and that the Bulgarians were going once again to foster the so-called Macedonian claims. …Tito himself has given the lead in various interviews and speeches in which he has gone out of the way to sing the praises of Yugoslav-Bulgarian friendship, and some of Tito's henchmen have gone yet further and publicly demanded Greek Macedonia for Yugoslavia. Meanwhile the Bulgarian press has announced a meeting in Belgrade between Yugoslav and Bulgarian delegates when the future internal political organization of Yugoslavia was discussed, on the assumption that there will be a federation into which Macedonia will also enter.[7]

Britain could not agree to a union or federation between Yugoslavia and Bulgaria, which would isolate Greece and almost certainly result in a drive to grab Western Thrace, Western Macedonia and the port of Salonika as the capital of a Greater Macedonia. Britain might, at the limit, accept the creation of a Macedonian state as part of a federal Yugoslavia, as long as there was no attempt to annex or lay claim to any Greek or Bulgarian territory. Eden suggested sending a warning to Russia not to interfere; Churchill wanted to avoid a clash with the Russians until stability was restored in Athens, despite the danger of communist domination spreading throughout the Balkans.

Pat's 'REPORT ON THE FREE MACEDONIA MOVEMENT IN AREA FLORINA 1944' was perfectly timed. On 11 December, at the height of the fighting in Athens, Rex Leeper cabled a summary to the Foreign Office for War Cabinet distribution:

1. A British liaison officer who was in the Florina area till November reports that the Capetanios of 2 Bn. 28th Regiment of ELAS, Gotchi, deserted with his whole battalion from the Vitsi area, near Florina, to Monastir in October, on being ordered by ELAS 9th Division to proceed out of their home area to Eastern Macedonia.

2. Gotchi is described as a boastful peasant with reputation as a good fighter. He and his men are all Slavophones and had long been suspicious of Greek EAM leaders even when disguised locally as SNOF. He is believed to be still at Monastir and some of his men are picketing frontier. He now signs as 'Commander of Kozani and Kastoria Brigade.'

3. Gotchi is presumably directly under Tempo, who is reported to have made a speech at Monastir on 10 November in the presence of a British and an American officer promising a free Macedonia, including Florina and Salonika.
4. Full report on conditions in Macedonia follows by bag.[8]

Foreign Office policy was based on official statements and press reports. It followed the Imperial tradition of maintaining a balance of power between competing national interests, taking little or no account of the region's ethnic, social, linguistic and cultural diversity. Whitehall believed that Greece had absorbed its Slav population and completely Hellenized Western Macedonia through the settlement of the Greeks brought out from Asia Minor in the 1920s. Evidence of the existence, aspirations and loyalties of large numbers of Slav-Macedonian villagers came as a shock. As the embassy's covering letter remarked, 'The Western Macedonian question thus appears to be assuming a rather different form from that hitherto contemplated' and 'transfer of the Macedonian Slavs would thus appear to be a more difficult problem than had been believed.'

Pat's report began the rounds in a Foreign Office file headed 'The Macedonian Question'. To their credit, officials were quick to recognize the value of first-hand information, even though it contradicted received wisdom. Denis Laskey of the Southern Desk called it 'An extremely good report.' A Mr Thomson added 'this is an extremely interesting document; unfortunately material on the Slavonic population of Western Macedonia is scarce and it is practically impossible to check much of the information given here.' On 16 January a third commented:

This report is most intelligent and interesting and informative. It is clear that, whereas a Serbian-dominated Macedonia had little attraction for the Slavs of the Kastoria-Florina area in Greece, the prospect of a genuinely autonomous Macedonia in Yugoslavia would attract them much... There appear to be two possible solutions for the area of Slavophones in Greece. (1) The union of the NW corner of Greece, including Florina and Kastoria and the Western shore of L. Ostrovo [now usually called Lake Vegoritis] to Yugoslav Macedonia. If the resultant injury to Greek interests is too great, then (2) a great improvement in the Greek treatment of these Slavophones. This solution would probably be highly satisfactory were there economic attractions in the area and were the Greek government to permit British or American capital to exploit those attractions, this bringing employment and impartial observers into the area.

On 19 January, a fourth added: 'The lukewarm attitude to Bulgaria is worth noting.' On 8 February, a copy was sent to Brigadier Fitzroy Maclean, who had been appointed by Churchill as the senior British liaison officer with Yugoslav headquarters in Belgrade, who was seeking assurances from Marshal Tito that the Macedonian brigades would not cross the border from Yugoslavia into Greece or cause any border incidents.

Fortunately for the Allies, Tito had more than enough to occupy his attention in the effort to cement the Yugoslav Federation and maintain his independence from Stalin. There would be no Macedonian insurrection in northern Greece. In a strange quirk of history, Pat's report was to surface more than forty years later, when it received wide circulation on the internet as 'an invaluable source for the study of the Macedonians in Greece, and, indeed, for the Macedonians as a whole' just as Yugoslavia was breaking apart and the Yugoslav Republic of Macedonia proclaimed its independence.[9]

Chapter Seven

Cairo: Intermission

A fter the Allied victory in North Africa and the German retreat from the Balkans, Cairo became a military backwater but the city remained rich from the wealth spread by the British Eighth Army and HQ Middle East. British officers and the better-off residents could still enjoy good food and drink, racing, riding, polo, theatres, concerts and an endless round of nightclubs and parties. Pat had a report to write, but once that was finished he was due for a month's leave, which he planned to spend 'lazing around Cairo, riding, dancing, talking Greek, writing, and playing the piano.' Now that he was away from Greece, he could write to Jill at length. He admitted that Greece had taken a heavy toll:

I had got pretty tired by the end of August, but there was no chance of a respite. By the middle of November I had had it: I was thoroughly tired mentally and physically, though not ill in any way; nervy and irritable, couldn't concentrate on work; could only sit around and talk all day; would snap and bark on any pretext. Now I'm a good deal better but still a bit flat.

He had a psychological boost when his CO put his name forward for the Military Cross. 'Don't get excited,' he warned Jill, 'I shan't get it. You need to have some outstanding exploit to your credit, not just steady work over a period. I don't mind; being recommended has bucked me up no end.'

Cairo's weather was lovely in December, with eight hours' sunshine a day, temperatures reaching 20°C and almost no rain. Absurdly, though, many of the shopkeepers had produced snowy window displays 'to tickle the fancy and empty the purses of the British' and the residents of the houseboat were nailing up pieces of cotton wool in an effort to make it look Christmassy. Pat was not amused:

Darling, in our Christmases to be, need we have any snow? I hate snow. I've had too much to do with real snow; tramped through it, fallen down on the ice underneath it or rocks half covered by it; had it in my boots; had mules get stuck in it and break their girths and damage their loads, had the wind coming over it freeze my ears and face. So I don't like being reminded of it.

I do *not* want a white Christmas. I want a brilliantly-coloured, vinous, blue-flame-pudding Christmas. Holly and mistletoe and masses of spruce boughs and some Christmas cherries and butcher's broom etc. – yes. Especially holly, whose berries I love. But *not* cotton wool, or any other ersatz snow. It reminds me of the real thing, which I can tolerate only when one uses it for winter sports.

Most of Jill's letters to Pat have been lost, but in those that survive she made light of hardships (she had been invalided out of the WRNS with what, years later, proved to be tuberculosis) and tried to entertain Pat with accounts of everyday life back at home. She was spending Christmas with her brother Jim (a geneticist), his wife Joan and their two small children, doing her best to keep up the seasonal rituals:

Pinner, 27 December 1944

Christmas has been very amusing. Joan & I spent Christmas Eve cooking heroically so that we shouldn't have too much to do on Xmas day & ended up tying up the parcels & filling stockings at 1 o'clock in the morning, having just got the cake iced, in a kind of stupor of sleepiness which meant that every movement involved ten unnecessary ones. The children woke at 6 the next morning in the best tradition, overexcited & all wanting each other's toys, but happy. Jane got the doll's pram she has been craving for & Polly an exquisite white teddy bear she adores, not to speak of endless less important dolls & books. We overate horribly on turkey & plum pudding & I spent the afternoon trying to sleep it off through Polly's screams (toothache). We put the children to bed early and spent the evening playing heads bodies & legs with shouts of laughter. Yesterday we had an elaborate tea with mince pies & a very ersatz Xmas tree decorated by Jane & myself. We had no glass balls or tinsel but by making stars out of coloured paper, cutting up big candles & wiring them on, twining white cards & rickrack ribbon in & out & throwing artificial snow over the whole we achieved a very pretty result.

Between Christmas and New Year, Jill made a trip into London to buy paints, check for mail at her own flat and look in on relatives and connections. Her descriptions, and the discussion of serious concerns in a tone of waspish levity, are redolent of Bloomsbury:

I went up to London alone, dashed around buying paints, looked in at 60A to see about letters, & went calling in Gordon Square. The Stracheys are back in force at 51 & I hoped to get news of aunt Dorothy who is still in France. I found Oliver (my great uncle), Barbara his daughter & at Oxford with me, & her child. Oliver, swathed in a great coat, was too busy eating turkey to do much talking – knew nothing & appeared to care less about his sister. But I daresay his bottles of whisky are much more important & in families of ten what is one sister more or less? Barbara was as loathsome as ever & still working for the BBC & her child talked without stopping – very sweet but backward. He loathes his school but Barbara keeps him there relentlessly. Why not try another? I went on to the Stephens & found Judith – the daughter – & her baby, sitting in a sea of nappies & cigarette ends waiting for the removers. Judith very gay & lively & the baby adorable, naked to the waist & blue with cold but happy.

Did I ever tell you about Barbara? She was the girl who was sent round the world on a windjammer to stop her marrying a man Oliver didn't approve, met a mad Swede on it & married him instead & had the unfortunate child. The Swede beat her & was got rid of by Oliver at great expense & Barbara then married the first man. A cautionary tale for all parents.

Gordon Square in Bloomsbury was built in the 1820s, with imposing terraced houses in brick and stucco grouped around a central garden. The Stracheys had moved into No. 51 in 1919. Oliver was brother to Lytton Strachey, the critic and biographer, and the youngest of the ten Strachey children to survive to adulthood; their father, General Sir Richard Strachey FRS, had been a Very Important Person in the administration of British India; their eldest sister, Elinor, was Jill's grandmother. Oliver's love of whisky did not prevent him from being one of England's leading cryptographers and living to the age of 84. Judith – five years younger than Jill – was a niece of Vanessa Bell and Virginia Woolf; Clive and Vanessa Bell's oldest son, Julian, who died in the Spanish Civil War, had been engaged to Jill.

Right at the end of the letter, Jill's light-hearted air slipped: 'Meanwhile darling the cable I had hoped for from you hasn't come & I can't help worrying but am trying to be sensible & blame Xmas traffic.'

Pat was mortified:

I feel an awful swine that you haven't heard from me, and one of my periodic cables failed to arrive. I'm frightfully sorry about this, and don't understand it. Nor do I understand why you haven't received an extra cable, over and above the fortnightly one, which I sent from Athens about 10 Dec.

He had moved out of the houseboat into a furnished room, which gave 'a pleasant illusion of domesticity' and was leading a very comfortable life, having drinks at Shepheards, going racing and watching polo at Gezira and Heliopolis. Heliopolis was the grander course, but Pat found Gezira more sympathetic:

> It's a tiny racecourse, on Gezira Island in the Nile; it looks like a croquet lawn set down on the typical desert island of the storybooks, if you can imagine that. Race meetings there always remind me of a garden party – although the men are dressed in uniforms (mostly battledress) and lounge suits (the Egyptians with beautiful crimson tarbooshes with a black silk tassel) and the women in simple frocks… The track encloses a golf course and a polo ground and there are lots of palms, looking as if they had been cut out of paper and stuck on.

After debriefing in Cairo, the officers and men of Force 133 were deployed to other duties. Some, including Leo Voller and Peter Kite, were sent to apply their wireless and explosive skills in special operations in South-East Asia. Although fit and well, Pat was no longer classified as 'Operational Personnel' on the grounds that he was over 30 and had experience that would be useful in post-liberation work; when he returned to duty it would be to apply his specialist knowledge of the Balkans in a non-combatant role. As a result of his report on Western Macedonia, he was urgently wanted back in Greece.

Greece had got under Pat's skin. Macedonia, its people, society and politics fascinated him and he felt he could make a contribution. He asked Jill, who was staying with an uncle and aunt in Cambridge, to

> Get on to some Cambridge don who knows something about the Macedonian problem – economic, territorial, political, agriculture, any and every aspect of it – and get him to give you a bibliography of books which constitute separate volumes on their own. Then take his list to Heffer, or send it to Blackwell, and get them to send me, instanter, whatever items on it they can provide. What I want is five or six books which will give a reliable introduction to the history and present condition of Macedonia, and the attitude of the various nations interested (Russia, Bulgaria, Britain, Greece etc).

Pat had been interviewed and recommended for employment by the embassy, which would probably lead to the offer of a post-war job. However, he decided to turn them down. 'I don't like Embassy people, what I have seen of them, and I don't like the Foreign Office either – experts in foreign affairs, which they ought to be, but a poor mentality.' After years in the army, he wanted to be his own master. 'Everyone is to a certain extent the slave of circumstances but why be the slave of an organization as well? Especially an organization one doesn't believe in – for that would be real slavery.' Moreover, he did not want to settle down in a foreign country, even Greece. Foreign countries were 'all very well to visit', but England was the place to live:

> What I look forward to our doing is settling down in England, with me teaching and writing for a start, then only writing... More and more, I lean towards the country, preferably near London, rather than to London or a provincial town. Better for the children; and one must have something earthy to do in one's spare time, a garden, and a pony or a sailing dinghy or something of that sort.

Like all SOE officers at the end of their mission, Pat had to complete a 'General Report'. For a writer, this was not so much a chore as an opportunity: the document that he finally handed in to the SOE office in Rustum Buildings ran to ninety pages. Pat was at pains to record the contributions of his men. Kite figured prominently throughout and Pat took pains to praise his radio operator, Leo Voller. 'The W/T operators in GREECE did excellent work,' Pat wrote, 'but I do not think any can have done better work than VOLLER did. He was outstandingly good at his job, under all conditions, and he had exactly the right temperament – keen and determined, and never rattled.' Pat concluded: 'I have been lucky in the people I have had under me. But in KITE and VOLLER I had two men who would have made themselves outstanding anywhere.' Their service in Greece did not go unremarked: in August Peter Kite was awarded the Military Medal and in September Leo Voller received the British Empire Medal.

At last, on 1 February, Pat could go on leave. Whereas in Athens he had been 'getting to know everyone', in Cairo he kept away from the embassy crowd and high society. He was happier 'drinking and talking of adventures in the mountains' with former SOE colleagues and wining and dining with a circle of Greeks that was 'quite undistinguished and consists mainly of employees in good posts.' This group included a Scottish-Greek girl, Mary, who had recently 'taken a knock from a boyfriend'. In his capacity as a temporary widower, Pat squired her around. He took Mary and her sister dancing to the Auberge du Turf. Mary was blonde and Kitty dark, and they both spoke English 'with a delightful foreign accent'. It was a successful evening, despite a moment when everyone was asked to talk quietly '*à cause de la radio-diffusion*.' The rumour of an armistice had been sweeping Cairo and everyone thought: 'This is it!' However, it was only the time for the band's regular Saturday night broadcast. The next day, Pat picked up a bundle of letters from Jill at the office, read them over dinner, and was so happy that he

> absorbed large quantities of brandy and ginger ale without noticing. All my fury at the stupidity of other people was sweetly washed away. You are a darling. What is this strange spell that you put on me? You are all the things that never came off in my life plus all the ones that did.

Jill was wise enough not to scold Pat or give any hint of jealousy about his doings in Cairo. Instead, her letters were full of love and solicitude, and on 12 February she wrote:

> My darling Pat, 15 letters from you arrived today, and I've been reading them more or less all day, feeling extremely happy and only wishing I could tell you in person instead of on paper how much I do love you, I have got complete faith in our future together, & it *does* make separation possible to bear, though odious. I don't feel it *can* be much longer now. We have just been listening to the report of the big three meeting & somehow it made peace seem so immediate & so promising that [we] wanted to go out & beat gongs or let off fire crackers, & having no alcohol, we had to rush into the kitchen & make cocoa furiously. …. Meanwhile it gives me enormous pleasure to think that you are having some leave, and drinking & eating camembert cheeses & sleeping all you want to & writing your poem & I hope you find a horse & a respectable piano. You write me such heavenly letters – you need never worry – goodnight dearest Pat & I love you. Your Jill.

They had now been apart for eighteen months and the physical separation was hard to bear. Pat wrote back:

> My thoughts about you, which pop into my head every hour of the 24 except when I am asleep, are divided into two classes according to mood: *a*, when I long for you, bitterly and emptily, and realize that even if I were to be unfaithful it wouldn't be the slightest use (it would be idle to pretend, after so long celibacy, that the thought has never crossed my mind) and *b*, when I think, in moments of hilarity and serenity, how incomparably fortunate I am in being yours and in you being mine, and how marvellous the future will be. In such moments I glow all over. At the moment, *b* is dominant but I suppose that, as usual, *a* will supervene before I go to bed.

Pat wanted to write a book about the war in Greece but needed time for the experience to settle. It looked as if his stolen notebooks and papers would be recovered, so there was no need to hurry to get things down while the details were fresh in his memory. He turned instead to his long poem, with growing excitement that it was going to 'come out, like a game of patience'. A fortnight later, he wrote hopefully that 'I've all but finished *The Burning Village*. I have a final section to write, perhaps two sections – probably two or three pages only – something that will resume and wind up the whole like a few chords on the organ.'

Riding in Cairo was a disappointment; the riding school instructors disapproved of the informal habits Pat had contracted in Greece, where

> one had one's own horse, knew him absolutely and rode with a loose rein, sitting in all sorts of unorthodox positions to prevent getting stiff. In the mountains it was looking after your horse that counted more than horsemanship – and I can honestly say that no horse of mine ever had a sore back.

Music was more satisfying: 'I went to a truly excellent piano recital the other night by one Ignace Tiegerman, a tiny Pole… Technically marvellous, and in feeling delicate and rich and sure. He played well throughout, but his Mozart in particular was quite astonishing; I have never enjoyed anybody's playing quite so much.' Tiegerman was asthmatic and had settled in Egypt for the climate; he performed and broadcast only rarely, but when he did it was a great occasion. For most of the time he ran a conservatoire, which Pat attended for weekly lessons with Mlle. Blanc, 'a very positive, rather intelligent and amusing young lady, an excellent teacher'. Pat was very gratified when Mlle. Blanc announced that she wanted to prepare him for an audition with Monsieur Tiegerman himself, '*parce que votre manière de jouer est vraiment intéressante.*'

It was not to be: February was drawing to a close and so was Pat's time in Cairo. He took with him a souvenir in the form of a green stone scarab, the sacred beetle of Ancient Egypt, the symbol of Khepri, the sun-god of daily birth and regeneration, which sits in front of me as I write.

Chapter Eight

New Beginnings? Florina and the AGIS

P at returned to Athens in spring sunshine. It was still chilly in March with snow on the nearest mountains, but the air was fresh and invigorating, 'not a raw windy cold like that of England'. The earth was bare and bleached but not barren, the colours were delicately tinted in the pale golden sunshine and the city was as magically lovely as ever: 'the scenery of Athens always gives the same sensation as being more beautiful than anything I have seen before, but not in the least wild or extravagant.' Pat was immediately back in the swim, making 'a host of new friends before having to go the rounds of all the old ones. Greeks, though often so brutal to one another, are almost uniformly welcoming to the casual stranger.'

A great deal had happened while he was in Cairo. In mid-December, British reinforcements had gained the upper hand and pushed back ELAS. Churchill had flown in to Athens on Christmas Day for a two-day conference; King George II had announced that he would not return to Greece until he was summoned by popular will; and on 1 January 1945 the Archbishop of Athens had assumed the Regency. Papandreou resigned and the Regent appointed a new prime minister, the elderly General Plastiras. ELAS finally overcame EDES and, in mid-January, agreed a cease-fire with the British. Following complex negotiations between the Communist Party, EAM and ELAS on one side, the government and the British on the other, final terms were signed at Varkiza on 15 February. The Varkiza Agreement was full of commitments to the steps needed to create a functioning democratic state, with pledges to uphold freedom of expression and trade union liberties; an end to martial law and a partial grant of amnesty for political crimes; purging and reform of the civil service and security services; the release of hostages; demobilization of ELAS and the surrender of an agreed number of weapons; and a plebiscite on the monarchy, to be followed by elections. How these commitments were to be delivered was another matter; nobody believed for a moment that KKE had given up.

On his return, Pat found a country in a state of shock, with

a complete lack of responsibility after nine years of Fascism (six of Metaxas, three under the Germans, and a pretty nasty dose of left-wing Fascism to finish up with). Everyone is afraid to take the initiative, rushes blindly into party discussion, about wildly unimportant things (e.g. shall the king come back – which is about as important as ought people to wear gardenias or carnations in the buttonholes; or should people wear caps or hats); and no-one will take a bold, national initiative on the basis of appealing to the real and good patriotism that exists in all Greeks and getting something done.

Plastiras was busy 'putting in all his friends – useless old men'. The city, though, was almost peaceful; there were a few shots and explosions in the distance at night, but the centre was normal.

Much as Pat might have liked to settle into Anglo-Greek literary life in Athens, he was now regarded as a specialist on the Macedonian problem and his work lay in the north. Britain was keen to organize the plebiscite and elections promised by the Varkiza Agreement as soon as conditions would allow. To help prepare the ground, Rex Leeper had set up the Anglo-Greek Information Service (AGIS) to provide information, give out news bulletins, help re-establish radio and newspapers, set up reading rooms and organize film shows. AGIS was not a cloak-and-dagger outfit, but it did gather information on military, political, economic and social conditions and events. Reports from regional offices were collated and summarized into a weekly briefing for the Foreign Office and War Cabinet. Both the communists and the extreme Right nationalists viewed AGIS with deep suspicion and saw its officers as the agents of British power.

In mid-March Pat made a short trip by sea up to Salonika, escorting a journalist, and a flying visit to his old haunts. He found himself greeted by old acquaintances who stepped off the pavement and pumped his arm up and down, beaming with smiles and saying 'Hello Captain', which was very gratifying, as was the prospect of what he described to Jill as another 'splendid Balkan imbroglio' that was brewing. By the end of the month, Pat was settling in to his new job with AGIS. His remit was to create and run a local organization in Florina, with a branch in Kastoria, operating up to the Albanian and Yugoslav borders to the west and north and across the plain to the east, liaising closely with the local state and church authorities.

Florina was the obvious place to establish a British presence: not only did it command the Balkan communication routes by road and rail, it was the regional administrative centre, with the prefecture and the seat of the Metropolitan. On the surface, it was an attractive little town, built in a wooded valley north of Mount Gioupka, just before the point where the River Sakoulevas flowed east into the plain. Most of the buildings were constructed of brick, stuccoed to look like stone in a neo-classical Ottoman style with carved wooden doors and attractive iron grilles protecting the windows. Next to the basilica, the bishop's palace was a grand neo-classical structure with a steep flight of stone steps up to an arched portico and entrance on the *piano nobile*, with a covered balcony from which the prelate could address a congregation in the square below. Villas and tavernas flanked the river as it flowed through the centre of the town.

As soon as he was settled in Florina, at the end of March, Pat wrote to Jill:

> Today my boss and I (one Geoffrey Chandler, a Captain like myself and an excellent man to work with) moved into our billets in a cool, well-built, local-style house which stands by a river on the edge of this little town (a town which I know fairly well) with a steep mountainside rising up directly behind the rear courtyard. It is said to be a good cool house in summer; as there is still snow on the higher slopes of the mountain it is a bit too cool at the moment and as I write this at 9 pm I have a glass of whisky (Canadian) and water beside me to keep up my morale. I'm in exactly the area I wanted and the situation is fascinating… I hope soon to get a horse; essential here, as some villages are inaccessible by any other means except one's feet…. The situation here is bursting with complexities and *I* (italics) *know* (ditto) how to deal with it (loud blast on own trumpet) and my hands are hopelessly full trying to cope and enlist the people who count (starting at the top) in getting things going.

Geoffrey had served in the Political Warfare Executive (a secret department closely linked to the Foreign Office and SOE) before transferring to Force 133 and landing in Greece in September 1944. After the German withdrawal, he became head of the Western Macedonian area of AGIS. Pat took to him at once: 'My immediate superior is a charming and amusing Captain (actually junior to me) with an excellent brain and plenty of guts under a cultured exterior. We get on just like that.'

A week after moving in, on 5 April Pat wrote again with a description of his surroundings:

> You'd love this house. It has clean board floors of softwood and big rooms which through being long can seem low but are not oppressive. At present it has pictures on the walls of the late owner shaking hands with the King of the Hellenes and an uncle, as a young man, in a French-style Greek officer's uniform of 1912 or thereabouts, and an amazing large watercolour, very *primitif* and rather inept called 'The Sheepdog'.
>
> The peasant women round here wear lovely and striking costumes, in which the effect is secured by a magpie arrangement of snowy white and pure plummy black. Of course there are other colour schemes which include royal blue and plum red and orange and lemon yellow and black and gold (in the form of jewellery and embroidery which come out on

feast days). There are storks and a broken minaret in this town. I am filthy, haven't had a bath for days. Must go to the local Turkish bath, which is tiny, looks like a mosque inside and a dilapidated cottage outside, and has a marble floor.

Western Macedonia was calm enough on the surface but still seething underneath with political, ethnic and autonomist tensions. ELAS had handed over the weapons specified by the Varkiza Agreement but many more remained hidden away. Pat was quick to reassure Jill about his safety:

> a very nice, straightforward and patriotic officer, who I am trying to get reinstated in the Greek army (he was in ELAS but not of it) said to me *à propos* certain villages I proposed visiting: 'Of course you know there are still guerrillas in those villages. But I can tell you without flattering you that the guerrillas admire and like you and there is no doubt they would never do you harm.'

I can still remember Pat telling a story, when I was a child, of being shaved by a village barber who had been ordered by a local communist leader to cut his throat. Fortunately, the barber thought that Pat was more powerful. The story gave me a lifelong fear of the old-fashioned cut-throat razor in the hands of a barber.

Early in April, the newly-formed National Guard arrived in Florina to 'a tremendous reception, in a carefree holiday atmosphere.' KKE appeared to be lying low, but there were threats of violence and 'a kind of quiet terrorism' in most of the mountain villages. Two different struggles were under way, one between KKE and everybody else, the other between Slav and Greek. Pat reported that outside KKE: 'there is probably not a single Greek who does not regard the British as the saviours of Greece – not only from the power of the left wing but also from the "forces of darkness" across the border.' Ominously, though, the Right appeared to be splitting into moderates and extremists.[1]

Prime Minister Plastiras lost the regent's confidence and resigned, to be replaced by another old warrior, Admiral Voulgaris. Pat, who was working from morning to night 'in a cloud of dust', wrote to Jill that:

> The Greeks are dreadfully slow at regaining a sense of initiative and national unity, the British are hard pressed for personnel and material, and are not very understanding, and the Americans are keeping themselves separate from the British and trying to sit on the fence ready for any eventuality, and doing their best to be friends with everybody in this internecine mix-up.

It was getting warmer and the Balkans were beautiful. Nightingales started to sing in Florina and soon the mountains too would be loud with their song; the garden was 'full of wisteria hanging heavy like bunches of grapes' and the river 'looked like iron and silver intertwined.' Pat made a trip to the Prespa lakes, which were as thrilling as ever, angry and stormy with white horses on the water beneath the snow-capped mountains. The marshes teemed with herons, egrets, pelicans (the wonderful Dalmatian pelicans, perhaps the largest birds on earth), buzzards, innumerable warblers, wild duck and geese. Prespa brought back Pat's memories of the year before:

> How beautiful, and how hopeless, and often how purely laughable our experiences were, we would trudge along the side of the lakes, and up and down the foothills and mountains surrounding them, and ride our horses at all hours of day and night, and I understand now we were taking in the strange intangible beauty of the place without knowing what it was all about.

Only KKE (by far the best-organized of all the political parties) was clear about its ends and means, but it was deeply distrusted; many people believed that the communists had tried to create revolutionary proletarians by causing villages to be burned by the enemy and by annulling savings. The extreme Right pushed the view that there were only two kinds of people: Nationalists (meaning themselves) and communists.[2] Easter was a time of rejoicing, but the celebrations were marred by a jittery feeling that the country was in a bad way: the traditional greeting 'a good Easter to you' was sometimes met by the rejoinder 'it is not a good Easter this year.' KKE was taking the line that 'Russia will intervene to help us soon and then you will be for it.' The Centre and Right were frightened by the possibility of war between Russia, the USA and Britain; they were afraid, too, that Tito might launch a push for a Pan-Slav Macedonian nation.

Economic confidence collapsed: the price of gold was volatile and inflation was rife. Florina's economy was closely linked to contraband across the borders with Albania and Yugoslavia. The Yugoslav partisan authorities had clamped down and reduced the trade between Florina and Monastir to a few horses, cattle and sheep:

> three men were recently hanged for possessing gold; another committed suicide after being deprived of all his goods and gold. On Good Friday a man from a village near Monastir took 300 lambs for sale in the Easter market: the partisan police confiscated all the lambs and distributed them to the people.[3]

Merchants from Florina took wheat and paprika to sell to their Albanian counterparts on the frontier, close to the village of Moshcochori. In May 1945 the price of paprika had risen to six times its pre-war level.

While KKE took advantage of the political and economic drift, 'visiting the plains villages by night, the mountain ones by day, encouraging the faithful and threatening the recalcitrant', the autonomist movement seemed to have shrunk to a small number of armed men on the hills. A small band was reportedly trying to raise a Slav-Macedonian rebellion on Mount Vitsi but the villagers of Polykerasos and Perikopi had been subdued by the ELAS purges of August 1944 and were in no mood for political adventure.[4] More worryingly, there was no sign of the kind of enlightened policy towards the Slav Macedonians that would lead to lasting calm and security. Pat was, once again, disillusioned and frustrated. He wrote to Jill: 'This life is driving me bats... My work has utterly palled. Running an information centre and doing news broadcasts in villages bores me stiff. The really important things, to me, are intelligence – military and political – which I am better qualified to do anyway.' Everything was tangled and muddled, and there were constant reminders of violence:

> an ex-mule-driver of mine who is accused of a murder he didn't do... came in here with the head gaoler to see me about getting bail. They are both Cretans; the head gaoler wouldn't have taken anyone but a compatriot out for a walk. I think I shall be able to fix the bail all right. I've been trying to get him out altogether but one doesn't know the meaning of the phrase 'the law's delays' until one has seen the Greek law at work.

A few days later, on 10 June, Pat went out to the Prespa lakes, where 'in one particularly wild, tangly and beautiful piece of country...the body of a villager was lately found in pieces. It had been done with axes at the instigation of the Bulgars. Really the Balkans are quite too Balkan.' He spent most of the day 'listening to a great many lies and a little truth about this and kindred events'.

On a more positive note, Pat opened 'a brilliant little reading room' in Kastoria, the other main centre of his bailiwick. Kastoria sits on the neck of an isthmus, surrounded on two sides by the waters of an emerald lake, ringed by mountains. The city was known in antiquity and its name is thought to derive from the Greek word for the beavers that flourished in the lake until they were hunted to extinction for their fur. Fur has been prepared and traded in Kastoria for centuries and Kastoria remained the centre of an international trade. The city's furriers were famous for their ability to match and sew tiny offcuts into an apparently seamless pelt, and many workshops as far afield as New York and Canada were founded by Kastorians.

Kastoria looked idyllic. Fine old Macedonian houses and Ottoman villas occupied the slopes of the hill, where the breezes from the lake tempered the summer heat. Pat's first impression was of

> a lovely place – big houses with white walls and crusty tile roofs, storks standing on the chimneys and chattering their beaks; trees and vines and roses and cool cobbled streets, steep and curved; a lake; and yellow and grey mountains and my own Vitsi, well over 2,000 metres high like a shark's tooth on the skyline.

The lake teemed with fish, and brightly-painted flat-bottomed fishing boats, with long-bladed oars mounted on heavy outriggers, added a picturesque touch.

Whereas Florina was Greek mixed with Slav, Kastoria was pure Greek which, together with its international connections, gave the town a wider outlook:

> Kastoria gets a bracing sense of unity from considering itself a Hellenic citadel, a northern promontory of the Greek spirit. These may seem high-flown words to apply, say, to an unshaven grocer happily mixing sand with his sugar and water with the wine in his shop on the hillside. But if one gets talking to any Kastorian, including the repellent grocer, one sees that under the surface this spirit of Hellenism exists, a real and brilliant thing. Much more real because it is more permanent than the whims and storms of party politics, which pass. It is a facet of Europe and the people know it in their bones.[5]

Pat opened the reading room in the presence of the bishop of Kastoria, the prefect, the mayor and more than fifty leading officials and personalities. The bishop ('a charming old man and more venerable than virtuous') made a speech and so did Pat. He sent home a (bad) picture of the occasion, taken by a local photographer. Pat is standing at the centre of the front row, between the bishop and the mayor (who is wearing a white suit). Everyone is smartly dressed, the buildings look fresh and well-kept and people are watching from the balconies, creating a sense of hope and quiet enthusiasm.

Pat soon came to realize that Kastoria suffered from its strategic position at the snout of the Balkans, combined with a poisonous climate and malaria-breeding marshes. For all its superficial charms, he thought, Kastoria would be 'unbearable to live in' with its 'cagey Turkish architecture, Greek small-town gossip and jealousy and a smell of Byzantine decay. Altogether just the place for the Greeks to live their idiosyncratic desperate life, the ideal setting for Hellenism.' Beneath the surface, everything was crumbling and the town was a 'sad and dusty relic of the splendour that was Byzantium.' In other words, it was only too Greek.

In June, the governor of the Bank of Greece, Kyriakos Varvaressos, published a programme for economic reform. Having been drafted into government as Minister of Supply, he launched a plan to cut inflation, control prices and collect taxes from the wealthy. Prices actually fell slightly; even the shopkeepers seemed to approve of the tax programme and generally paid up. However, terrorism continued to flourish, there were not enough troops to keep order, both the National Guard and Gendarmerie were beating up suspects, the prisons were full and the authorities could not cope.[6] The officer commanding the Florina Gendarmerie, Major Ioannou, was a good man, 'quiet and reasonable, imbued with the idea of justice, intelligent and clever' who agreed that 'if you treat the Slavophones well, as Greeks on an equal footing with other Greeks, they will become Greeks. If you do the opposite they will become Bulgars.'[7] However, Pat was sure that he would never be given a chance to solve the Macedonian problem:

> All the heads of department in this town are horrible little hell-hounds, incompetent, unjust and spiteful in the Greek manner. They will either swamp him or else intrigue against him and throw him out. And there are all the other towns and districts in Northern Greece where Slav is spoken and there is a Macedonian problem to be solved. I'm trying to ride it all easily, like a cork, and take nothing seriously, and renounce all my hopeless ambitions of influencing the course of affairs here.

The officer in charge of the Gendarmerie's security department had no interest in seeing justice was done but only wanted to make arrests. He would not allow Slavophones to speak their language in the streets or market, but wanted to entice them down from the hills so he could swoop and arrest the lot.

A handful of civilians had set up a secret organization in Florina called the Union of Macedonian Strugglers or EMA (which spoken meant 'blood') whose objective was counter-terrorism and the liquidation of the leaders of 'pro-Bulgar' organizations. In the red corner, EAM was now talking about 'the third round' and saying 'wait till the British leave.' Pat wrote to Jill on 6 July that 'all the bad things the Left have done – mostly paralleled by the bad things the Right have done – have come up into my mind; and my mind is black.'

Britain's July 1945 General Election was a great distraction: the Greeks looked on the poll, and Churchill's defeat, almost as a Greek affair:

> Today has been rather disturbing: the election results coming through in breathtaking instalments and the Greeks (who are simply a mass of

error) twittering with fright as the Labour total mounted up. (Not *all* the Greeks: the Communists and, here in Macedonia, the pro-Bulgars are delighted, but afraid to crow too loud.)

A touring theatrical troupe from Athens presented a witty, salacious and highly political review. Praise of Russia drew loud applause from the back of the hall and the gallery; praise of Greece drew loud applause from everywhere. Condemnation of internal Greek conflict was applauded 'with the same heartfelt sincerity that Greek civil wars have been conducted in the past and will be in the future.' One sketch illustrated 'the peculiar quality of most Greek anti-Semitism' being at once both friendly and heartless, mingled with a regard for the Jews' smartness. Violence in the mountains was increasing, and armed bands were reported to be operating in close connection with the Yugoslavs across the border, with deaths and disappearances at a rate of one a day.[8]

Pat and his team were making the best of the summer, the fruit and the fine weather. For a dinner with the prefect (the district's senior administrator) one of Pat's staff, Alek Zrek, 'concocted a marvellous drink by grating peaches and pears and squeezing the pulp and mixing the juice with gin. It completely removes the morbidity from gin and you go on drinking and drinking it till suddenly you find you are somewhat drunk.' Pat went swimming in the lakes near Amindeo to the east of Florina and Alek arranged horses to go riding, together with Nat Pilides, the interpreter, who had 'spent years with the British Army in the last war and being a true Balkan character knows six-and-a-half languages.' Nat's mother came from Pisoderi, near the borders with Albania and Yugoslavia. Pisoderi was a pretty village with a lurid history. Papastavros Tsamis, the village priest and son of a wealthy Vlach merchant, had played an active part in the Greek–Bulgarian struggles over Macedonia until in August 1906 he was lured to a clandestine meeting in the woods and hacked to death with an axe. Nat spoke Vlach just as easily as Greek, as well as Macedonian and Turkish, and fairly good Serbian and Bulgarian. When Geoffrey Chandler visited at the beginning of August, they all went for a picnic lunch with bread, bully beef, tinned salmon, tea and ripe peaches and pears. They chilled the peaches and pears under an ice-cold spring that came out of a small iron pipe in the hillside; the water was delicious but too cold to drink in large quantity.

However disappointing the venture in wartime Greece had been and however frustrating the present, Pat found the experience was deeply interesting and, ultimately, worthwhile:

Life in England, any rate in peace time, was so regular and decent and honest and prosperous that one just didn't learn how villainous people are, how much more advanced and humane England is than most countries and how *vraie et criminelle* is the life of most other people in most other countries.

Pat had developed a warm affection and respect for his colleagues. Nat was widely travelled and vitally interested in life, with delicate manners and feelings. Pat found him quite unaffected, 'full of spirit, gay without being foolish, and steady but nothing of a puritan.' As a known Anglophile, Nat had had to hide both from the Germans and from the communists; he had a lucky escape when an American bomb dropped on the Gestapo Florina headquarters just days before he was due to be arrested. During the occupation, Nat had become destitute and ended up going barefoot: when his savings were exhausted, he had sold his ring and his wife's jewellery for wheat to make bread. In March 1945, when Pat hired him, he was wearing an ancient dinner jacket made of English cloth because he had nothing else. Alek had been arrested and interrogated by ELAS, ostensibly for having 'kept company with rich people' in Athens but in reality because he was working for the British. He was fortunate not to have been murdered, but released after three and a half months' imprisonment in appalling conditions. Another of Pat's connections told him how a friend of the family had been betrayed to the Germans during the occupation by a Bulgar:

> the Germans arrested him and fifteen minutes later he was shot dead. The Bulgar thought it prudent to retreat to Salonika. Old Grigóri said: 'If it was any relation of mine who had been killed the matter would have ended differently. I would have gone to Salonika and found a man and said, how much do you want? Fifteen pieces of gold? Twenty? Take them!' That is, he would have hired an assassin. He told me this in a moody way which made me hold my breath, it was so natural.

The pace of work slackened in the summer heat and Pat sometimes found time to write:

27-ish August

It is half-past ten and so far I have done no work. I've been re-reading your letter, reading Stefan George, and have just written a poem.

European Lake
A little calf with leather throat
Eating maize stalks from a boat
Under the sunlight's golden bell
Beside the crystal of a well.

The boat is up, the nets are dry,
No dead fish now with frightful eye
Accuses the fisher of his trade
Which Adam drove, Jehovah made.

Instead, the idle nets like sun
Hang on the posts; the shore is dun,
The fearful grey of years of life,
Summers', winters', autumns' strife.

It has dry glimmering sounds and scents,
This lake which mimics innocence.
Here many murdered and begot them
Those, as many, who forgot them;

Who, beneath the church-bells' sound
Which lays its nets of silver sound
With orange jackets, clarinets,
Fall each one too in someone's nets.

The lake was Prespa; the people in the last verse were getting married 'and were going to beget and murder and "just live" like the others'.

Throughout September, October and November, Pat continued to type out, adjust and send Jill instalments of *The Burning Village*, a poem (or series of poems) in eighteen sections about war and its savagery. 'It solves no problems, reaches no ultimate conclusions, and points no way out. The position is simply one of acceptance – without conceding one iota to the beasts, Hitlers, dogs or false prophets. Which, I think, is the only conclusion worth reaching (after all Shakespeare never got any further).'[9]

A constitutional plebiscite and General Election seemed no closer. Varvaressos' economic recovery plan met so much opposition that he resigned at the start of September. British officials in London found it more difficult than ever to see how a stable democratic leadership might emerge. The traditional parties were run by discredited survivors from pre-war days, who had played no part in Greek politics for a decade. The communists, who had dominated the resistance, were well-organized but deeply distrusted and the attempt to form an all-party government under Papandreou had been a dismal failure.[10] As the moderate centre disintegrated, politics became polarized between the extremes of Right and Left. Pat explained to Jill, in a letter written from Florina on a fine autumn afternoon, that:

In Greece there is nothing like our Labour Party, which attracts the left-wing element of the country and renders it harmless; the Communist Party is the only effective left-wing organization and in addition the rich of Greece have almost no sense of responsibility towards their workers, on whose labour their wealth is founded, and for the most part do not even begin to understand that the only way in which Capitalism can render Labour innocuous is to treat it well and give it the square deal in life which is the right of every man. I have rarely met a class of people for whom I have less respect than the Greek rich – though they are delightful to meet at dinner, and have charm and wit above the ordinary. Add to their short-sightedness and rapacity the fact that the Greek temperament is as hot as paprika and turns naturally to extreme and violent measures: on the Right to repression, on the Left not so much to revolution in the full and organized sense as to insurrection and troubles, which may not get very far in actual results gained for the workers but tend to diminish security and to keep the rich as heartless as before. So weak is the cause of constitutional Socialism in this country that during the special conditions created by the Occupation, and skilfully exploited by the extreme Left, even a number of the peasants were induced to take a passing interest in Communism, though most of them were shrewd enough to realize that Communism was simply a new kind of tyranny which did not chime well with the permanent interests of the small owner of land.

With the rare exception of the occasional fine day, autumn formed a grey interlude between summer and winter, with no light and the sound of falling leaves, which Pat – in an echo of Charles Baudelaire's poem *Brumes et pluies* (*Mists and Rains*) – found 'very funereal and pleasing'. He was glad to be in the town rather than in one of the high mountain villages where even the summer had been interrupted by torrential rain and hail.

On 5 October, after prolonged wrangling, Admiral Voulgaris announced that elections would be held in January 1946, before the plebiscite (not after, as agreed at Varkiza). A storm of protests broke out, and he resigned. It would be many weeks before a new government could be cobbled together. A mood of pessimism took hold as the Greeks became convinced that war between Russia and the Anglo-Americans was inevitable, which would cause the currency to collapse. Gold was the only alternative to the drachma and no one kept drachmas if they could help it. Although gold was not legal tender for transactions between private citizens, the police were powerless to stop everyone using it. Demand for gold pushed up the price: the official bank rate for the gold sovereign was 4,000 (new) drachmas, the equivalent of £2 paper, but the actual rate in Florina was 36,000 drachmas. The inflated price of gold in turn pushed up the price of commodities. For example, the beautiful, heavy, shaggy mountain blankets cost about 25,000 drachmas, which was more than £12 sterling at the official rate, but well under a sovereign in reality; the pre-war retail price for the same blanket would have been £2 or less. As a result, it had become economically impossible to export goods from Greece to England. Florina itself had been impoverished by the reduction in trade with Albania and Yugoslavia.

Economic deterioration and the procession of ephemeral governments encouraged the Greek nationalists to dream of re-establishing national pride through a war to push back the frontiers across the mountains into Albania and Yugoslavia. On the other side, there was an actual threat to security from Macedonian autonomist bands and armed *Ohrana* supporters in the villages. The *Ohrana* was an Axis-sponsored pro-Bulgarian organization, which was active in both Yugoslavia and Western Macedonia; the Greek branch was based in Florina. After the Axis defeat, many of the *Ohrana* threw in their lot with the Macedonian Liberation Front. Seventeen people were arrested in Kallithea on the eastern bank of the Prespa lakes and charged with aiding an autonomist band; another band was reported to be in the hills a few miles south of Florina.

During the war ELAS and KKE had assumed – and KKE continued to believe post-war – that Pat, as a British officer, was a man of the Right. They were mistaken: like many intellectuals of his generation, Pat himself had joined the Communist Party in the 1930s, as an Oxford undergraduate, and had read Marx and Engels. His membership did not last long and his experience in Greece removed any lingering desire to join the Labour Party. By 1945 he defined himself as a Radical – emphatically not a Tory but 'a leftish Liberal' – although he had no idea what being a Radical meant in terms of British party politics. At heart, Pat was intensely curious, open-minded and suspicious of dogma. Refusing to take conventional ideas on trust, he was interested in people as individuals, irrespective of their class, status or occupation. He believed that

> when all is said and done, people living together peaceably under their own roof, and producing families and doing something productive – whether it be turnips or sonnets – are and always will be the basis of civilization and are of themselves doing something towards the peace and wellbeing of the world.

> Most ideas about the world, *Weltanschauengen* [*sic*] and what not, indeed all such ideas or syntheses which I have encountered, are one-sided and insufficient, and do less than justice to reality which is many coloured and changing and inexhaustible.

In the case of communism, he objected not so much to the political theory as to the 'cruelty and violence and crookedness, which are the basis of much of the substance of the Communist movement in this country'. Politics were essentially less important than banking and finance, and what mattered most of all were individual lives and activities:

> Political problems – the really important ones like justice and a good life for all, or the atomic bomb – are never solved, even in a country like England, which is fairly sane, though we do get a pretty good, patched up solution, in default of a radical permanent solution. The only thing one can do is live a peaceful, pleasant life, which harms no-one, and be constructive if one can. In that way one is at least adding to the life of mankind, not taking away from it. In my belief, to write stories or make frocks *is* constructive and I've no urge any more to 'do good' or do 'something useful' in the ordinary sense… And the only action which is completely satisfying and leaves no aftertaste of frustration is creation. Almost anything can be creative, from making love to wasting time. Life in general, as far as I can see, is completely pointless – like nature – and may be meaningless into the bargain.

Macedonia continued to throw up new experiences. On 21 October 1945, Pat became the godfather to the youngest daughter of one of his former mule drivers, Andonis, at a ceremony in the village of Flambouro. Pat and Andonis settled on the name 'Betty', 'the height of exoticism to provincial Greek ears'. The church was stuffed with icons (a mixture of the old and dusty with the new and gaudy) and packed with people. The priest gabbled his way through the litany as fast as possible, but everyone enjoyed the service, which was 'rather rowdy and jolly, like so many things Greek'. Pat had to hold the baby for what seemed like hours and was terrified he would drop her:

> Fortunately she slept all the time except during the actual anointing baptism, which was a hot bath in a large pewter font, when she screamed the church down. And at the end of the service everyone shouted together: 'always to be honoured as godfather' which is apparently customary but seemed very nice of them.

As the godfather – and in keeping with his status as a local dignitary – Pat provided all the proper presents and the baby clothes. After the service, he had to 'walk at the head of an informal procession, carrying the child, with everyone in their peasant Sunday best (much of it embroidered) emerging to the front door of their courtyards and saying "May the child live" as we went past.'

Andonis had been the chief of Pat's former mule drivers; four others (Petros, Kosta, Lakis and Christos) also lived in the village and it would have been an insult to refuse hospitality from any of them. So Alek, Nat and Pat each had to eat as much as five men, and the day turned into an ordeal by 'fiery *tsipouro*, rather new vino, and huge helpings of pork, chicken, potatoes, apples, new wheat bread and a great deal of walnuts'.

Pat went back to Flambouro a month later for 'a consecration service about some Greeks who were slaughtered rather picturesquely by the Bulgars nearly two years ago.' His group first went to Andonis's house, where baby Betty was fast asleep but woke, howling. All Pat's old mule drivers turned up and a lively party began, with a great deal of wine, pork and pie. Several people dropped in with petitions, which he couldn't satisfy but this hardly seemed to matter:

> If you receive the supplicant with a calculated mixture of ceremony and familiarity they are almost as pleased as if you actually solved their problems. The great thing is to talk to them and above all get them to talk, so they expend their worry even if you can't remove the cause. As for the mixture of ceremony, the purpose is to make them feel you are an imposing personality, a man of power (this is the Balkans) but nevertheless out of your great goodness and wisdom, prepared to talk simply and sympathetically – which shows you are a very great man indeed.

Two hours later, the party rolled merrily away to meet the Boy Scouts at the village school, just round the corner from the church:

> The Scouts were very eager and well-washed and looked (quite deceptively) as if butter wouldn't melt in their mouths. The rear of my retinue was brought up by one of my mule drivers, Kosta, who was by now quite fuddled. He took it into his head that it was his duty to greet us all ceremonially, although the (very sober, rather peeved) village president had already done so quite correctly. So he shook hands with everybody and ended up by beaming at the whole company and saying in a loud voice 'Fuck 'em all.' He doesn't know what it means but is immensely proud of the expression and uses it on all occasions. The scoutmaster then made a long speech about everything, including party politics and the necessity of killing Bulgars. He then showed us all round the school, and I kept saying 'yes' and beaming. That done, we set about the baked meats and everyone made speeches, including me, and also Kosta who was by now seeing double.

The weather was bad and the Greek dignitaries failed to appear: Pat had to go back again (and make yet another speech) the next Sunday, when 'all the Greeks wept and snuffled in church.' A Greek brigadier sat next to Pat and whispered a story, bubbling with laughter:

> Once in the last war at the front we captured some enemy positions, I was a captain then. I went to sleep and had a marvellous dream – I dreamt I had a beautiful girl in my arms and I woke up, it was morning, and it was a captain I had in my arms. Ha ha ha. An enemy captain. Dead. You see we had captured the position by night, after all.

Florina was still one of the most sensitive areas in Greece, strategically located at a Balkan crossroads that dominated a much wider region. Some of the inhabitants turned towards Greece and England, others towards Bulgaria and Russia. Pat set up a school in Florina, both to meet the demand for English teaching and as a way of increasing British influence. Nat Pilides was placed in charge as secretary and succeeded in establishing the school despite the difficulties: there was no official funding, few qualified civilian teachers and no money to bring them in from further afield. Fees had to be extremely low to make sure that people could afford them. To start and then close for lack of sufficient numbers would have made a worse impression than not to have started the school at all. Thirty of the 200 pupils paid nothing, the rest paid just 300 drachmas – less than the price of a packet of cigarettes – for eight lessons a month. Fortunately, the premises came rent free and, despite the low charges, the school was self-supporting.[11]

At the beginning of December, Nat presented Pat with a small package and a card with birthday greetings in English: 'From Nat Pilides: To my dear Captain P.H. Evans.' In the package was a pair of cufflinks and a bracelet and a butterfly brooch for Jill, 'all filigree silver and, with the exception of the brooch, very Byzantine in feeling. The bracelet is of broad square links and being entirely filigree is as light as air. It would go with dark silk or velvet.' Nat's gift pleased Pat very much, although it gave him a pang. In spite of his salary from AGIS and his meagre profits from the English school, Nat was still poor.

Midwinter, with its heavy snow and long nights in the run-up to Christmas and the New Year, was a time for celebrating, reflecting on the past and looking to the future. It snowed hard for days at a time, and the town became still, cold and luminous. Pat went skiing and, at Alek's instigation, to have his fortune told:

> One snowy afternoon the three of us tramped up the riverside to one of the cottagey quarters. Up an alleyway through a pandemonium of tobogganing children; down some earth steps into a small yard thinly

surrounded with frozen palings; up a rickety wooden staircase which leant sideways against a leprous pink wall and ended under the eaves; and into the house, which was like the shoe of the old woman. Tiny windows with patched panes; a general air of huddle and of squalor without dirt; children and darkness everywhere. We were hastily ushered into an adjoining room, small and dull and gloomy, something like the parlour of an English labourer's cottage on a winter's day. A brazier was brought and the woman came in with a pack of cards.... The next day we had another fortune-teller, this time bringing her here as she said she had just killed a pig and her own house was upside down in consequence. This woman had a different method. She sat down by the stove with a plate and a glass of water. On the plate was a lighted candle shining through the glass. Out of her bag she took a tiny ebony cross and clicked it several times on the rim of the glass, making the sign of the cross after the orthodox fashion (top, bottom, right, left). Then she dropped the cross into the water, looked at it as it lay in the radiance at the bottom of the water, and started talking. She told me that a man with fair blond hair, name beginning with K, had been working against me for the past two years, first as a military person and now as a civilian, and that he would shortly make a definite attempt to do me harm. This attempt would take the form of writing a letter, to which I would not reply, and would fail.

It was a fascinating performance but the prediction was not completely convincing. The only person Pat could think of who might fit the description was his former chief spy, Kostas: 'a Communist, a wild resentful boy and the world's most assiduous double-dealer – though by no means the most intelligent'. Although Kostas was hostile to the British and buttered them up purely for his own advantage, Pat did not believe there was any personal hostility. Exploiting the British was a Balkan habit and a fact of life. Pat had a natural sympathy with people on the wrong side of authority; the trouble was the Greeks took the cheating too far. As he prepared to leave Florina, with a mixture of disappointment, regret and relief at the prospect of getting away from a town he found increasingly claustrophobic, Pat reflected on the Greek and Balkan dilemma:

It's a vicious circle; the merchant evades his taxes; the civil servant is underpaid and takes bribes from the merchant; the collaborator collaborates and after the liberation bribes witnesses and lawyers and gets off scot-free and has a good time on the black market. And so it goes on. It was the normal condition before the war and will go on for years untold. It is customary in the Balkans. Of course the people who suffer most under such conditions are the poor and also the educated young without much prospects; hence Communism which finds in these two classes of discontented people its politically exploitable masses and its unscrupulous and fanatical leaders. All the countries which have quasi-Communist regimes now are simply paying for the irresponsibility and political bankruptcy of their ruling classes before the War.

On the face of it, the new dispensation, however brutal, is the new broom which will sweep clean – sweep away all the old men, the rottenness, the bad habits. But I doubt it. Habit is everything in the Balkans; even revolution is a habit; and men don't change. I should not be surprised to see in a few years that the new regimes in Bulgaria and Yugoslavia are as rotten as the old – certainly they are as brutal and perhaps more so. Greece, of course was the one exception; there the leftward swing was arrested by foreign intervention and something vaguely resembling a pre-war regime installed. I think that in the long run Greece will come out better off than her neighbours, freer and happier. If she doesn't, it will be her own fault.

Chapter Nine

Going Home

By the winter of 1945, Pat was desperate to get home but the question remained: how would he earn a living back in England? Late in November, he had an interview in Salonika with two officials from the Ministry of Information (the wartime government department for publicity and propaganda), who offered him a job as the ministry's Greek specialist in London at a starting salary of £660 a year; he would have the option of either making a career as a permanent civil servant or dropping out after a three- or four-year term.[1] The offer came out of the blue and Pat accepted on the spot. The men from the ministry would apply for his immediate release from the army and with luck he would be home in January. After closing down the operation in Florina, which would take a fortnight, he could go to Athens to wait for embarkation. It seemed almost too good to be true.

Pat arrived back in Florina on 1 December, his 32nd birthday, and wrote to Jill the next day in a state of euphoria to say he was coming home to be married.

Before leaving Florina, Pat gave away his belongings to people who had helped him and he presented Andonis – the father of his goddaughter Betty – with a mule.[2] This was a significant present: giving a Greek villager a mule then would be rather like giving him a tractor now. By the end of December Pat was on a Liberty ship, slipping down the Thermaic Gulf from Salonika to Athens. Getting away had involved the usual muddle. The night before he was due to leave, Pat was up until 2.00 am or so, writing official letters and packing. He set his alarm for 6.30, but when he woke it was bright daylight and his watch said 8.10. Embarkation was to be completed by 9 o'clock and he was nowhere near ready:

So I pulled on my clothes, dashed out unwashed and unshaved, and gave the movement order and all the embarkation cards except my own to the rest of the party. They trundled off in a truck towards the dock quarter. Having made my own preparations I got a jeep and a driver and an Irish trooper who is normally drunk but who is rather attached to me, and set off at a wicked speed – hoping we wouldn't meet any M.P. patrols, as they are rather hot on the speed limit. We had gone only half a mile when we met the truck coming back, with the party still on board. The boat, so far from leaving Salonika, hadn't even reached it. So we trundled home again and I ate a leisurely breakfast and shaved and spent a day of comparative rest. So today we had another shot… To walk, to chatter, to smoke and eat and lounge, on a hollow steel box which goes vibrating over scarcely rippled waters, gives a curious sensation of freedom and leisure; there is nothing one can do except enjoy it.[3]

As Western Macedonia – 'that magnificent, claustrophobic place; a rugged arena on a gigantic scale, without edges' – receded into the distance, the feeling of constriction vanished. Seeing a review of Durrell's book about peacetime Greece, *Prospero's Cell*, made Pat impatient to get *The Burning Village* into print as soon as possible and write his own book about Greece under the occupation. However, the latter would be a long job:

> I can't just write a plain record of events like a ship's log, I have to have an imaginative grasp of the subject before I begin; partly because it will be a consideration of values as much as a narrative of events; and partly because I have to make up my mind about those events and the issues which they raise and, in one or two respects, about myself also.

Driving up from the port of Piraeus, he suddenly felt

> the old exquisite emanation of Athens come welling up to meet me, as fresh as ever. It's like the flower called amaranth, unfading. It's a feeling that everyone is walking about a foot off the ground and that in some sense when you enter the fringes of the emanation you will start doing the same. (You do.) A feeling that everything inessential is shorn away and no longer exists; that every man and woman in the place is individual; man, as wise and foolish and crazy and passionate and eternally empirical as man, as such, ever was; and immemorial, yet never quite growing up. A feeling too that even the children are wiser than other children and wiser than they themselves know, and naughty, and charming, and a bit bad. A feeling that something is beginning for you.[4]

Pat was writing to Jill on a fine, soft, blue Athenian winter day, with a powdering of snow on the distant mountains and a view of the Acropolis across the tiled rooftops. Living in Athens had 'a queer effect, like a drug, and a stimulant at once, so that one feels anything may happen to one and one may find oneself doing anything under the sun'. Pat whiled away the days of waiting by reading, writing, talking and drinking in nightclubs until the small hours. Athens offered a wide range of cultivated company, British as well as Greek, including the novelist Rex Warner, who was head of the British Institute, and Osbert Lancaster, the press attaché at the British Embassy, who was 'even more witty and intelligent than one of his own cartoons'.[5]

Then things started to go wrong. The men who interviewed Pat in December had failed to send the signal to London confirming his acceptance of the offer, and London had appointed someone else who was 'much less acquainted with Greece, and in addition can neither read nor speak the language'. To make matters worse, the War Office had clamped down on early releases. A big shot from the Ministry of Information had turned up in Athens and offered to fix Pat up with a job in London, but only on condition that he would stay in Greece until the end of April. Pat would be sent back up to Salonika as press officer attached to the Consulate General. If he made a success of the job, a job in London would follow; if not, it would be back to the drawing board. It would not be easy in Salonika, with 'chaos and cold weather and not nearly enough staff; and *everything* to be organized from scratch'. Despite the disappointment and the pain of the prolonged separation, Pat was sure it would be the right decision for both of them: a job in 'the propaganda side of the Foreign Service' would provide enough money for them to live on amusingly, was something Pat could do successfully, and would not stop him from writing:

> 'Don't think that my deliberately putting off my return home is coldness, or any doubt about us,' he wrote. 'If I had ever had any doubt about us, since that moment in 1943 when I suddenly realized I wanted to marry you (and said so), our life would have split us apart long ago. As it is, nothing whatsoever can split us apart, ever.'[6]

Salonika brought promotion to major and the chance to explore a great and ancient city that had been founded in the fourth century BCE and named 'Thessaloniki' after a sister to Alexander the Great. In the context of the kingdom of Macedon, Thessaloniki was a new town, which had survived and prospered while earlier cities disappeared. Thessaloniki was ruled first by the Greeks, then by the Romans, Byzantium and the Ottoman Turks before becoming the second city of modern Greece. When St Paul preached to the Thessalonians, there was already an important Jewish community, which played a major role in the city until liquidated by the Nazis. The variations on the city's name reflected its many communities: it was Saloniki in popular Greek speech, Solon in Slav, Selanik in Turkish and Salonika (from the Jewish Ladino dialect) or Salonica to foreigners. Officially restored to Thessaloniki after the defeat of the Ottomans in 1913, the new, old name was slow to catch on.

After a visit the previous October, Pat had described his pleasure at stumbling across the Arch of Galerius, the Roman gateway on the original border of the town, with its marble frieze through which trams passed on a single track. A stone's throw away stood the Rotunda of St George, built by the Emperor Galerius as his mausoleum towards the end of the fourth century CE, converted into a church by the Emperor Constantine, used as a mosque by the Ottomans, and reconsecrated as a church in 1912. Just beyond the arch, sunk in the earth like an air-raid shelter, was 'a small Byzantine church like a cluster of old-fashioned bee-skeps joined together.' Pat had wanted to get to know Salonika better, not only the antiquities and centre but also the charming spots 'crying out to be painted' tucked away in the endless suburbs, which 'simply reek of Greek history and bitterness and childish gaiety'. Now he had a privileged position above the Leoforos Nikis, the bustling promenade that runs along the quay, from which to observe the doings of 'this exhilarating rat-hole'. In the distance, across the bay, Mount Olympus and Mount Kissavos glistened in the cold winter sun or loomed, ghostlike and threatening, under clouds.

Travel, wartime experiences and wide reading in French, German and Greek had made Pat 'nearly as much European as British' and given him a great respect for 'the curious ways of foreigners'. His first official dinner guests, in early February, were the editor of the town's right-wing Liberal paper, 'an intelligent and most entertaining man' and the second-in-command of the local Reuters bureau. Despite the ouzo, good food and the wines, conversation never quite took off. Pat was exasperated by his colleagues' inability to speak anything other than English:

> Really, why *can't* people learn languages and also let their minds go a little?
> Schoolboy French is enough; lots of people whose job entails sociability
> get on well with that; it's only a matter of having a ready tongue and
> plunging ahead. Greeks are not at all stuck-up about languages and are
> admirably ready to meet anyone half way if only he is prepared to have a
> go. Just now, I distrust the English environment and education with all
> my heart, as a means of forming presentable human beings. It tends to
> build backbone and character but not humility, grace, wit and warmth;
> it breeds stiff, clumsy people who cannot unbend because they've never
> started doing it, and in many cases don't want to, at any rate where
> foreigners are concerned. Damned arrogance.

A few days later there was a party for Gracie Fields, who was amusing and charming and not in the least affected; the next night was a consul general's dinner party with the governor general, the supreme military commander of Macedonia and other bigwigs.

Jill was house-hunting in London. Pat wrote to encourage her to take decisions for both of them. He was 'working like hell' but thriving on it; partying and drinking in Athens had got rid of the pent-up frustrations of Florina and now he was much happier, working for his own and Jill's future. Unfortunately, Pat's letters from Salonika were delayed in the post. Jill had had no news since he left Athens and was furious. Pat replied immediately to justify himself and reassure her:

20 February 1946

Darling, you must be crazy. Did you or do you really think that I have been taking all you are doing for granted?

It was quite natural you should be jealous; one gets that way sometimes, with long absence and so on. And it was a good thing you took the lid off: much, much better than keeping it on. But what you haven't realized is that I had to take the lid off too, in the sense of having to go and carouse. It was pretty tense carousing and at times almost hysterical. I don't think you realized how bottled-up and really how fed up with life I had got in those trying nine months in Florina… I was missing you badly and had to find relief and distraction somehow. Hence the nightclubs. You wrote, why not miss one out now and again? Frankly the answer is that I couldn't. I reached the state when the only times I didn't go out to dinner and then a nightclub were either when I was too physically tired to face staying up in a shrieking fug till four in the morning or else when I was near being broke. On those occasions I used to sit in the bar at the Minerva Hotel and drink myself into a drugged condition which would enable me to go to sleep; without it I should have lain awake for hours, feeling more horrible than I could bear to contemplate. I had to have alcohol or fatigue or both. I was missing you very badly and am doing so now. Up here, work has taken the place of dissipation. But even here there have been plenty of evenings, indeed most evenings, when I have sat here at my desk, sometimes writing to you, sometimes reading Greek, sometimes working and occasionally writing a poem, with a bottle of brandy to keep the emotions quiet…

Don't be alarmed, by the way. I'm not developing into a real soaker. I drink just enough to bemuse myself, and only in the evenings, and not every evening at that. Tonight I have had nothing but an ouzo before dinner and a merely social glass of wine after it.

Will you get it into your head that I love you?… The only thing that can make either of us happy is to be together again, and letters are just hammering at a wall when it comes down to this sort of thing.

Suddenly, the mail got through and Jill received twelve letters all at once. She spent a day reading and re-reading them, replying in a letter full of relief and love, all the rage washed away. Why bother about ministries, official posts and flats in London? If only Pat could come home at once, he could get a job as a teacher, they could live in the country and raise children and keep chickens and be happy anywhere, as long as they were together. However, the complicated dance with the Ministry of Information continued. On 4 February, Pat had received a signal offering him a post in London 'almost certainly to do with Greece'. Then another arrived, dated 16 February, saying: 'Deeply regret post in Greek Section will not be available when you return for demobilization and we will see whether an alternative will be available.' Pat had had enough and replied – quite untruthfully – that he had now been offered another job elsewhere. He would not delay his demobilization but he would come to see them when he was back in England.

On 3 March 1946, Pat left Salonika for the last time. In Athens, waiting for a ship to England, he reflected on his feelings of exile. In the future, he would have to learn to live in his own country and to feel 'united to my own soil and home, our own cities and countryside' despite its privet hedges, hypocrisies and conventions. Walking in the wild Keramikós cemetery, the ancient cemetery of classical Athens, he picked up

> an inch-and-a-half fragment of a pot, or urn, with a crisscross geometric pattern in *sang-seché*, that smoky *sang-seché* which is so lovely. It will look pretty on our mantelpiece; it will be both useless and valueless, and will always be a piece of the sun and of Greece.

Hanging around felt like 'being in a railway waiting room for hours and hours without a book'. Athens, though, could never be really dull, particularly since he had fallen in with the circle surrounding Lulu Metaxas, daughter of the Greek dictator:

> Lulu Metaxas is a curious person, electric and fine, like a squirrel; very amusing, quite mad and quite Greek. I find her alternately irritating and enchanting; she is completely a child, but with all the wit and fire of a grown woman. (To 'child' should be added the epithets 'sparkling' and 'perverse'. In looks she is like a monkey.) She has a string of lovers (they run successively, not concurrently) and holds wild symposia at which the behaviour is informal but perfectly decorous and the talk is forked lightning until four or five in the morning. And she is madly in love with her own country and spends long hours reading the memoirs of the makers of the 1821 revolution (the War of Independence) and the *Song of*

Songs (in a beautifully smooth translation). Which explains perhaps why she is still unmarried. Any man who got hitched up to her would either be foolish or superhuman, because he would have married a country not a woman, a cause incarnate. In politics she is probably dangerous, if she counts for anything at all. She is said to be carrying on some sort of activity with a most frightful crook called Nikoloudhis, who was Minister of Press and Publicity in her father's regime. Lulu, however, is a very good person to know, in small doses, on a purely social plane. I count myself lucky that I was invited to three of her symposia.

Pat had given up worrying about jobs: he would have three months' paid leave after demobilization and something would turn up, either at the Foreign Office, Ministry of Information or the British Council; teaching was a last resort. All he wanted was to get married as quickly as possible. His kit was packed and ready to load at the reception camp, leaving him and his toothbrush at the Grande Bretagne, the best hotel in Athens, which had been taken over by the embassy. Day by day he expected to go; day by day the journey was put off. Finally, it was settled: he was to report at the reception camp by eleven o'clock in the morning on 21 March and the boat would set off the same day; he should reach London at the beginning of April.

Epilogue

Jill and Pat were married by special licence in Hampstead Registry Office on 4 April 1946. Jill had found a flat on the entrance floor level of a tall, cream-painted stuccoed villa at 16 Buckland Crescent, between Belsize Park and Swiss Cottage. Buckland Crescent is a street of substantial houses with steps leading up to double front doors, set back under porches supported by Ionic columns. Inside No. 16, the high-ceilinged rooms were filled with light from tall, wide windows, which had retained their original shutters. A balcony ran across the back of the house, with an iron spiral staircase leading down into a garden with a mature fig tree.

There they settled to make a home and a life together. Pat decided that they must have a piano. He went with Jill, her best friend Frida and Frida's husband, Brian Easdale, to Harrods' piano hall. Pat and Brian – a professional pianist as well as a composer, who would win an Oscar for the score of *The Red Shoes* – went from piano to piano, gathering an audience, before settling on a Bechstein grand. The piano swallowed up most of Pat's gratuity and unspent pay, but the Ministry of Information had come up with the offer of a job. As Films Officer Western Europe he would have enough to live on and start a family, and so it was that I entered the world two years later, on 20 May 1948.

It was not long before Pat found life as a civil servant unendurable after the freedom and excitement of the war. Offered establishment and a career, he resigned and went to work on the night shift of the Walls ice-cream factory. One day, he disappeared. Jill told me that he would 'come back very soon, with the golden guineas jingling in his pocket'. The fairy tale image stuck in my mind, but now I think that Jill was reassuring herself as much as me.

I must have been 3 years old at the time. Not long afterwards we moved to a cottage in the countryside near the hamlet of Crown East in Worcestershire, where Pat had accepted a job in a preparatory school. Fifty years later, I went back for the first and only time: the cottage was empty, overgrown and dilapidated, but otherwise almost unchanged. Crown East had no shop or pub, just a farm, a little church, a parish school and a gaggle of houses. Stuck down a country lane in a primitive cottage, 5 miles from the town of Worcester and without a car, with a small child and a cat for company, Jill cultivated her garden, grew fruit and vegetables, and kept chickens. With Pat's encouragement, she began to write and became an author, publishing fiction and children's books under the pen name of Polly Hobson.

Pat was a sympathetic and inspiring teacher but the school was dreary, the hours were long and the pay poor. In a fit of depression and to Jill's undying regret, he destroyed the unpublished manuscript of *The Burning Village*, along with all his other poems. He never returned to Greece. Although he loved that most brilliant country, its people and language, he had invested too much frustrated hope ever to go back. Ten years before he died, Pat suffered a disabling stroke. After that, he gave up any idea of writing about Greece. He handed over his wartime diaries, signals and reports (but not his private correspondence) to his former commander, Professor Nick Hammond, who lodged them in the Liddell Hart archive.

Jill and Pat were unable to have more children, but the marriage was a lasting success. I still have the wooden breadboard given them as a wedding present, with their names and the date carved around the edge: I use it, and remember them, every day.

ॐ   ॐ   ॐ

On 30 March 1946, the eve of polling for the long-delayed Greek general election, a communist band descended from Mount Olympus and attacked the town of Litokhoro. The third and most terrible round of the civil war raged from the autumn of 1946 until the ultimate victory of the National Army, with American support, in 1949. All civil wars are terrible; as Pat had predicted, the fight in the mountains was conducted with brutal savagery and atrocities that have left their scars on the people and the landscape. Western Macedonia, which had suffered so much from the occupation, was finally devastated.

The National Army burned Vapsori in 1947 and in 1948 the government evacuated the mountains to prevent the communists from recruiting or conscripting villagers; Vapsori was abandoned and never resettled. In the 1950s even its name was wiped out and the cluster of ruins on the mountainside was renamed Pimeniko. A once thriving and populous village had been caught up in a world war that was none of its making before being swept away by a civil war in which both sides professed high ideals. The forces of the Left had preached the rule of the poor and dispossessed but the villagers' simple lives were destroyed. Handsome stone houses on the spiny mountainside were left to ruin among orchards and meadows abandoned to the hunting hawk and its cowering prey.

Korifi, Pat's old staging post on the heights of Vitsi, to the north-west of Vapsori, has also been abandoned; so have Trivouno, Pili and dozens of other villages that he knew. Moshcochori still exists as a name on the map but nothing remains on the ground save for a few tracks on the mountainside. Kallithea and Dendrochori fared slightly better: both were abandoned and destroyed during the civil war but were rebuilt and resettled later.

A mountain region that was once full of people is now almost empty and most of the surviving villages – even those with an air of prosperity – are dying. Almost all the inhabitants of Pendalofos are old and many of the well-kept houses belong to retired people who only come in the summer or at the weekends. There is nothing to keep the young there; at the last census, the death rate was nine times the birth rate. People have gone to the towns, but even Florina, Grevena and Kastoria have declined and the urban fabric is shockingly dilapidated. Many of Kastoria's fine old Macedonian houses and Ottoman villas stand empty; almost all of them are crumbling and decayed.

Dotsiko, with its elegant stone bridge, gives an impression of prosperity but it is a ghost village: only a handful of people live there in the winter. In the August holidays, scores of the former inhabitants return to open up their barred and shuttered houses and the population briefly mushrooms. Nestorio and Polykeraso, too, are ghost villages, maintained by grants, pensions and remittances.

What of the people? Pat's friend, John Mulgan, had won the MC in Thessaly and been promoted to lieutenant colonel. After the Germans left, Mulgan went back to Greece to carry out 'the melancholy task of trying to find and compensate those people who had been killed or crippled fighting for us during the occupation'. On 26 April 1945, shortly after returning to Cairo, Mulgan was found dead in his hotel room from an overdose of morphine. Various explanations have been advanced to explain his suicide, without solid evidence: loneliness, distress and the shadow of depression weighed dangerously on creative spirits. He left behind a manuscript *Report on Experience*, which was published posthumously by Oxford University Press in 1947.

Arrianos and Yannoulis became commanders in the Communist Party's 'Democratic Army'. Yannoulis was held responsible for failing to hold a vital position in the battle of Mount Grammos in 1948, was tried by a people's court and executed. Arrianos escaped north; after years of wandering and exile behind the Iron Curtain, he returned home to his native village. Rennos, too, fled Greece in 1949 and lived in East Germany, Romania and Hungary. He returned after two decades and received a pardon from the military junta that ruled Greece from 1967–74. He found that even the regime of the colonels offered more freedom than East Germany or Romania, renounced communism and became an advocate of 'direct democracy'. As a result Rennos was ostracized by both Right and Left and was largely shunned by his family (who felt he had abandoned them); his funeral went almost unattended.

The mule driver Andonis returned to his hometown of Charnia in Crete when Betty – Pat's goddaughter – was a few years old. In 2010, she was still living there with her husband.

Pat is still remembered in Western Macedonia. In Pendalofos I was told 'he was famous, a figure in history'. In Flambouro it was the same: 'Captain Evans was an important man, he is in all the books about the War and Civil War. The men of the Left did not always write kind things about him, but everyone respected him.' 'He was a great man; he was famous for his fairness and correct dealing; even the Left respected him.' 'He never left any debts, but paid for everything in full. He was a gentleman. All the British officers were gentlemen and everyone knew the women were safe with them around, which was not true of all the other guerrilla leaders.'

Members of the Guinis family still live in Avyerinos, where they own a substantial café on the village square. Philippos' adopted daughter was living in Thessaloniki in 2013.

I met Christos Dalamitros, the last survivor of Pat's muleteers, in Florina in 2010. At 95 years old but still alert and quick-witted, Christos remembered his time with Pat as the best of his life. For many years the former muleteers used to visit the ruins of Vapsori to show their friends where they had been with Captain Evans and tell their grandchildren about Pat and their exploits. 'Light a candle on his grave for me when you go home,' Christos said, and that is what I did.

Endnotes

Chapter One: The Journey Out

1. From Pat's notebook, LHCMA 1/6.
2. As remembered by Gerald Durrell and quoted in *Gerald Durrell: The Authorised Biography* by Douglas Botting, 1999, p.58. Gerald Durrell described this period in his autobiography *My Family and Other Animals*, in which Pat appears under the name 'Peter'.
3. Pat's SOE personnel file, National Archives HS9/489/9, notes that he had been in Greece from August 1936 to January 1938 and walked from 'Ioannina to Verroia'. He is wrongly described as having studied at St John's College Cambridge (rather than St John's Oxford).
4. HS9/489/9.
5. From a diary note in LHCMA Evans 1/6.
6. SOE personnel file HS9/489/9.
7. The diaries and letters of Lord and Lady Amberley, edited by their son, the philosopher and mathematician Bertrand Russell, published by the Hogarth Press in 1937.
8. LHMCA Evans 2/1/7 from Appendix J of P.H. Evans *General Report* January 1945.
9. LHMCA Evans 1/1.
10. Squadron 148 Record of Events for September 1943, National Archives AIR 27/995/19.
11. LHCMA Evans 2/1/7.
12. LHCMA 1/2, Pat's diary notebooks for 31 October–November 1943.

Chapter Two: Boodle

1. Prentice *General Report*, National Archives HS5/691.
2. John Koliopoulos, *Plundered Loyalties*, New York University Press, 1999, pp.99–100.
3. Prentice *General Report*, National Archives HS5/691.
4. P.H. Evans *General Report*, LHCMA Evans 2/1/7.
5. National Archives CAB/66/43/18.
6. Described by Nick Hammond in *Venture into Greece*, p.104, and recalled in Pendalofos in 2008.
7. LHCMA Evans 1/2.
8. Telegrams between Boodle (and other mission stations in Greece) and SOE Cairo are in The National Archives HS 5/483 'Greece Relief Supplies and Compensation'.
9. The description of the village deputations come from Pat's notebook LHCMA 1/2.

10. Signal from Boodle to Cairo, 29 November 1943.
11. P.H. Evans *General Report*.
12. Signal from Boodle to Cairo, 30 November 1943.
13. Mark Mazower, *Inside Hitler's Greece*, 1993, republished 2001, p.80.
14. Noted by Pat, and published by Hammond in *The Allied Military Mission in North-West Macedonia 1943–4*, Balkan Studies 31, Thessaloniki 1991.
15. *General Report* by Major Ronald Prentice, LHCMA Prentice/Wickstead 2/5/1.
16. Leeper to Foreign Office, telegram 396, 19 December 1943, National Archives file HS 5/220.
17. C.M. Woodhouse, *The Struggle for Greece 1941–49*, p.80.
18. Foreign Office telegram 2204 to Moscow, 8804 to Washington, 22 December 1943, National Archives HS 5/220.
19. Moscow to Foreign Office, telegram 1624, 25 December 1943, National Archives HS 5/220.
20. Leeper to Foreign Office, telegram 400, 28 December 1943, National Archives HS 5/220.
21. Anthony Eden to Mr Balfour in Moscow, 29 December 1943, National Archives FO/954/1A.
22. Balfour to Foreign Office, telegram 1654, 30 December 1943, National Archives HS 5/220.
23. Foreign Office to Leeper, telegram 320, 28 December 1943, National Archives HS 5/220.
24. LHCMA Evans 1/3, which contains Pat's diary from 20 January to 19 February 1944.
25. Diary note, 24 January 1944.
26. Diary note, 29 January 1944.
27. As told to the author by Professor Mikos Diakakis, a cousin of Rennos, who remembered Rennos in Athens in the 1970s.
28. C.M. Woodhouse, *The Struggle for Greece 1941–49*, revised edition 2002, pp.64–5.
29. P.H. Evans *General Report*.
30. Dated 17 February 1944, LHCMA Evans 2/2/10 and published in N.G.L. Hammond, *The Allied Military Mission in North-West Macedonia, 1943–44*, Balkan Studies 32, Thessaloniki 1991.

Chapter Three: Fertiliser: The Station on Vitsi

1. For more on the *Komitato* and formation of the *Komitadji* see Koliopoulos, *Plundered Loyalties*, p.58 ff.
2. From P.H. Evans *Introductory Report on Sub-Area Vitsi*, 7 August 1944, LHCMA Evans: 2/1/4.
3. LHCMA Evans 1/2, diary note November 1944.
4. LHCMA Evans 5/3-5 contains records of payments.
5. Signal of 9 April 1944.

6. J. Koliopoulos, *Divided Loyalties*, pp.125–6.
7. From *Introductory Report on Sub-Area Vitsi*.
8. *Vitsi Report from Dendrochori, P.H. Evans to Col. Edmonds*, 9–10 April 1944, LHCMA Prentice/Wickstead 2/1/2.
9. See J. Koliopoulos, *Divided Loyalties*, p.125.
10. Interview with Christos Dalamitros, the last of Pat's muleteers, April 2010.
11. From a signal forwarded to Cairo by Edmonds, dated 18 May 1944, LHCMA.
12. From R. Prentice *General Report*, LHCMA Prentice/Wickstead 2/5/1.
13. Pat's *Report on the Free Macedonia Movement in the Area Florina 1944* gave the number as 'about 300'. His *General Report* written some weeks later put the number at '120, I think, but this is from memory.'
14. Letter to Edmonds, 25 May 1944, LHCMA.

Chapter Four: Special Operations

1. Evans *General Report* op cit.
2. Christos Dalamitros, April 2010.
3. N.G.L. Hammond, *The Allied Military Mission and the Resistance in West Macedonia*, Institute for Balkan Studies, Thessaloniki 1993.
4. Christos Dalamitros, April 2010.

Chapter Five: NOAH'S ARK

1. *Introductory Report on the Sub-Area Vitsi*, 7 August 1944. The original is in The National Archives, FO 371/43764; a copy, retained by Pat, is in LHCMA EVANS 2/1/4.
2. The change of command and control of the Allied Military Mission is described in N.G.L. Hammond, *The Allied Military Mission in North-West Macedonia 1933–44*, Balkan Studies 32 p.126 & ff, Thessaloniki 1991.
3. Tozer *General Report*, HS5/691.
4. Chapman 'Report on activities in No 1 Area, Period Sept 8 to Dec 23 1944', National Archives HS5/690.
5. Report from Evans to Prentice, 19 September 1944.
6. Evans *General Report*, Appendix E, 'Disaffection in Enemy Forces' and the problems caused by Cairo's policy over surrenders.
7. LHCMA EVANS 2/1/6 and 1/4.
8. Signal to 'Pompforce', the incoming British army forces, 14 November, quoted in N.G.L. Hammond, *The Allied Military Mission in North-West Macedonia 1933–44*, Balkan Studies 32, pp.141–2, Thessaloniki 1991.
9. Captain Tozer *General Report*, National Archives HS5/691.
10. Gerry Livieratos *General Report*, National Archives HS5/691.
11. Contained in Prentice *General Report* LHCMA Prentice/Wickstead 2/5/1.
12. Archives of Modern Social History, Athens, KKE Regional Committee of Florina 415/23/8/248.

Chapter Six: Separatism and Civil War: the Macedonian Question

1. Mark Mazower, *Inside Hitler's Germany*, Yale 1993.
2. National Archives FO 371/43649; there is another copy in FO 286/1159, together with covering letters from the Athens embassy and an Appendix that was not sent to the FO.
3. FO 954/11B/328.
4. FO 954/11B/329.
5. Prentice SOE personnel file HS9/1209/5.
6. FO 954/11B/336.
7. W.P. (44) 707, now filed in The National Archives as CAB/66/59/7, Memorandum by the Deputy Under-Secretary at the Foreign Office, Sir Orme Sargent.
8. FO 371/43649.
9. Andrew Rossos, 'The Macedonians of Aegean Macedonia: A British Officer's Report, 1944', *Slavonic and East European Review* (London) 69, no.2 (April 1991):286.

Chapter Eight: New Beginnings? Florina and the AGIS

1. AGIS Weekly Report No 28, 22–29 April 1945 in FO 371/48269, 'date of information 2–8 April 1945'.
2. AGIS report for 22 April–5 May 1945, now in LHCMA in the papers of Geoffrey Chandler.
3. Pat's AGIS report for 6–19 May 1945.
4. Pat's AGIS report for 20 May–2 June 1945.
5. Pat's AGIS report for 17–30 June 1945.
6. Pat's AGIS reports for 3–16 June and 1–14 July 1945.
7. Pat's AGIS report for 17–30 June 1945, LHCMA.
8. AGIS Weekly Report No. 41, July 22–28 FO371/48276; Pat's AGIS report for 15–28 July 1945, LHCMA.
9. Letter of 4 October 1945.
10. Briefing from the Southern Desk to the Foreign Secretary, 5 August 1945, FO371/48276.
11. AGIS report for 3–17 November 1945, LHCMA.

Chapter Nine: Going Home

1. Letter of 29 November 1945.
2. Interview with Christos Dalamitros, April 2010.
3. Letter of 30 December 1945.
4. Letter of 6 January 1946.
5. Letter of 10 January 1946.
6. Letter of 26 January 1946.

Select Bibliography

There is a considerable literature, written from a wide range of different perspectives, on the history of the SOE in general, the activities of the SOE in Greece, the occupation, Macedonian independence movement and Greek Civil War. The following brief selection of English-language sources gives priority to books by participants in the action but does not list the many scholarly articles consulted by the author for background and cross-reference in support of the primary sources:

Chandler, G., *The Divided Land* (Michael Russell, Norwich, 1959; revised 1994)

Cooper, A., *Cairo in the War, 1939–45* (Hamish Hamilton, London, 1989)

Foot, M., *SOE: An Outline History of the Special Operations Executive* (revised edition, Pimlico, London, 1999)

Hammond, N., *Venture into Greece* (William Kimber, London, 1983)

—— *The Allied Military Mission in North-West Macedonia 1943–4* (Journal of Balkan Studies No. 32, Thessaloniki, 1991)

—— *The Allied Military Mission and the Resistance in West Macedonia* (Institute for Balkan Studies, Thessaloniki, 1993)

Koliopoulos, J., *Plundered Loyalties* (New York University Press, New York, 1999)

Koliopoulos, J. and Veremis, M., *Greece: The Modern Sequel* (Hurst, London, 2002)

Mazower, M., *Inside Hitler's Greece* (Yale University Press, New Haven & London, 1993)

Mulgan, J., *Report on Experience* (Oxford University Press, Oxford, 1947)

Woodhouse, C., *Apple of Discord: A Survey of Recent Greek Politics in their International Setting* (Hutchinson, London, 1949)

—— *The Struggle for Greece, 1941–49* (Hart-Davis McGibbon, London, 1976)

Index